RURAL DEVELOPMENT

Learning from China

SARTAJ AZIZ

HOLMES & MEIER PUBLISHERS, INC.
New York

First published in the United States of America 1978 by

HOLMES & MEIER PUBLISHERS, INC.

30 Irving Place, New York, N.Y. 10003

Library of Congress Cataloging in Publication Data

Aziz, Sartaj.
    Rural development: Learning from China

    Bibliography: p.
    Includes index.
    1. Rural development—China. I. Title.
HD2097.A97 1978   309.2′63′0951   78–489
ISBN 0–8419–9371–9
ISBN 0–8419–0372–7 pbk.

Printed in Hong Kong

About the Author

Sartaj Aziz is currently Deputy Executive Director of the United Nations World Food Council and was Deputy Secretary-General of the World Food Conference held in Rome in November 1974. From 1971 to 1975, he was Director of Commodities and Trade Division in the Food and Agriculture Organization of the United Nations (F.A.O.).

He was born in Peshawar, Pakistan, in 1929 and was educated in Punjab University (Pakistan) and at Harvard (U.S.A.). For a good part of his career, from 1961 to 1971, he has been with the National Planning Commission in Pakistan. In 1969 he spent a year at the World Bank in Washington to assist the Pearson Commission on International Development. In December 1976 Mr Aziz was elected President of the Society for International Development.

He first visited China during the Cultural Revolution, in December 1967, as a member of a Pakistan economic delegation which went to China to seek Chinese economic assistance for Pakistan's Third Five-Year Plan. His second visit was in February 1973, when he accompanied the Director-General of the Food and Agriculture Organization to discuss China's re-entry into the Organization. His third visit, in October 1974, was in his capacity as Deputy Secretary-General of the World Food Conference in order to discuss China's participation and role at the Conference. His fourth visit, in August 1975, was specially arranged to collect material for this book.

This book has been written entirely in his personal capacity and does not in any way reflect the views of the organisations for which he has been or is working.

Acknowledgements

I completed the first draft of this book in the summer of 1976 at the Institute of Development Studies, University of Sussex, in the United Kingdom. I am particularly grateful to Richard Jolly and his colleagues at I.D.S. for their assistance and intellectual stimulation. Richard Conroy and Binya Shrestha of the I.D.S. provided valuable help in collecting and compiling statistical information on China and other countries. Audrey Hugget very patiently typed the first draft.

I received extremely valuable comments on the first draft from Shahid Javed Burki, John Cairncross, Ronald Dore, Scarlett Epstein, Johan Galtung, John Gittings, Richard Jolly, Michael Lipton, Hans Singer, Benedict Stavis and Jonathan Unger. I wish to thank them most sincerely.

I would also like to express my warm appreciation to my secretary, Jennifer Parise, for her untiring help in preparing the final manuscript.

Finally, I am most grateful to my Chinese friends and hosts for their warm hospitality during my successive visits to China. They spent long hours in explaining the Chinese system, answering questions and providing whatever information was readily available.

My debt of gratitude to Barbara Ward is already very heavy. She has added to this by writing such a perceptive Foreword. Her remarkable vision of the problems facing mankind and her deep commitment to humanity will continue to provide guidance and inspiration to all those who are seeking solutions to these problems. She summed up the basic dilemmas that face the world today in a remarkably simple manner when she wrote to me in December 1976, after receiving the manuscript of this book:

> Your book arrived this morning and was the nicest Christmas present – of course I would be honoured to write you an introduction. Meanwhile I will try to send any comments that

seem relevant on the applications of the Chinese model. Remembering my beloved Africans with their infinite preference for chatting, singing and dancing – and the lovely long spells between harvests that make these delightful human pursuits possible – I would expect a keen cultural hesitation and one which, I confess dear friend, I shamefacedly share! But the obverse side is dead babies, the failed harvest, the life without safeguards. Yet what is so discouraging and disgusting is what Western man has made of his 'safeguards'. Have you seen the full figures I simply hinted at the triage article in the NYT? (*New York Times*, 15 November 1976.) It is that the West Germans spend 2% of GNP or $13 billions a year trying to undo the effects of over-drinking and over-eating – the beer-sausage syndrome. This really isn't far from the vomatorium! – BARBARA.

SARTAJ AZIZ

Contents

List of Plates

Foreword

by Barbara Ward

It is perhaps the supreme paradox of late-twentieth-century development that the chief success story in all the nations' varying strategies of growth and change should have been achieved by the nation which rejected 'the conventional wisdom' of both Left and Right and evolved its own uniquely effective response.

No one contests China's quarter-century record of economic growth, social advance, conquest of inflation and unemployment and a sharp decrease in the rate of growth of the population. In fact, as Dr Sartaj Aziz makes clear on the basis of what are probably the most reliable figures that can be pieced together, the Chinese have found solutions to virtually all the major problems posed by the first stages of modernisation – problems which have left all too many other nations caught in a trap of economic and social contradictions. And now comes the sobering fact. This Chinese achievement was contrived by ignoring the accepted beliefs of Western development experts and the most sober tenets of orthodox Marxism. It is no small record to have reached success by the route which nobody else had even thought out, let alone recommended.

Dr Aziz gives us an absorbing account of the process. It was inevitably and sensibly one of trial and error and, particularly between 1957 and 1966, experiments were continuous to establish the right size for an effective farm unit – the larger 'production brigades' and, within them, the village level 'production teams'. Much experiment went into the evolution both of the size and the function of the overall instrument of local government – the commune. But in this twenty-five years of learning and experimenting, the first and basic decision – highly non-Marxist and non-Western – was precisely *not* to give priority to industry – least of all, to heavy industry – in order 'to absorb the surplus rural population' – but, on the contrary, to give the first priority to agriculture and use its growing productivity for local diversification.

Within this overall strategy Dr Aziz distinguishes five central themes which, in his belief, have converged to produce China's remarkable rates of economic growth and social advance. These are: equitable distribution of rural land and resources – in other words, the abolition of large holdings and the absorption of small farmers and landless families into cooperative farm structures; the collective organisation of all farm families to work on supporting activities, above all, in irrigation and measures against erosion; diversification into a wider range of work as new needs emerged, work not only related to food production (fish farming, orchards) but to the industrial activities required for farming; the steady extension of basic programmes of health and education and, perhaps the most vital of all, the creation in the commune, the 'production brigade' and the 'production team' of local instruments of joint action which could effectively work within the larger framework of the Chinese economy without losing either their autonomy of decision-making or control over the surpluses their work had built up.

How did one country break every intellectual and social precedent and go on to succeed where others failed? Admittedly, it is the world's oldest continuous civilisation with all that this implies in discipline, intelligence and trained manpower at all levels. But other ancient societies are still floundering. The fundamental achievement was Mao's. After the Shanghai debacle in 1925, he saw that China's industrial proletariat was too weak to make a revolution. Abandoning Marxist orthodoxy ('the idiocy of rural life' and so on), he turned to the 80 per cent of the people who were peasants. For instance, one of the extraordinarily effective techniques on the Long March was to take a group of peasants prisoner in each area, allow them to spend a time of comradeship and discussion with the marchers and then release them, knowing infallibly that a Maoist cell would be left behind as the March went on. Nor did the Army strip the land; on the contrary, it helped the harvesters. Long before 1949, the primacy of the peasant was established and after 1949 not even all the Soviet's brief period of aid and advocacy of industrial priorities could shake the basic decision.

But Mao's decision can be both explained in historical terms and seen as the basis of sufficient support in popular terms because of the unique conditions in pre-Communist China. Dr Aziz's vivid picture of the abject misery and hopelessness of the Chinese peasantry is the only proper and convincing introduction to the breakthroughs since achieved. As Dr R. M. Tawnay, a perceptive British traveller of the 30s commented:

> A large proportion of Chinese peasants are constantly on the brink of actual destitution . . . a propertied proletariat which is saved . . . when it is saved . . . partly by its own admirable ingenuity and fortitude, partly by the communism of the Chinese family. . . . It is, however, true that over a large area of China, the rural population suffers horribly through the insecurity of life and property. It is taxed by one ruffian who calls himself a general, by another, by a third and when it has bought them off, still owes taxes to the government. . . . There are districts in which the position of the rural population is that of a man standing permanently up to the neck in water, so that even a ripple is sufficient to drown him.

This picture, brought back by one of the greatest economic historians of his day, gives us two main clues to the later Chinese revolutionary experiment. For the vast majority of the peasants, life was so intolerable that Mao and his marchers and the new communal experiments in Communist-controlled territory were the last lodestone of hope, the last chance of keeping heads above water. Mao's revolution had probably the most massive popular support in history.

The second clue is 'the communism of the Chinese family'. The villages had a millenial tradition of aiding each other and working together. Mao had the wisdom to use this cultural inheritance. It is significant that the 'production team' is pretty well the equivalent of the old village community. And it has been evolved as a basic working tool by trying out various sizes, groups and systems of reward. No dogmatic Stalinist mass collectivisation ruined the rural structure. It was almost nudged into place by successive steps and perceptive responses. Similarly, with the commune, it could draw on a decentralised provisional tradition but it has been remoulded and rethought and reshaped to become an instrument of effective integrated development, largely self-supporting and self-financing and hence drawing on the enthusiasm or at least acquiescence of those who actually do the work.

The question of China's suitability as a 'model' for other nations' development raises two issues before all others. The first lies beyond the scope of Dr Aziz's admirably comprehensive book. We do not yet know how China will deal with the social and economic problems of more advanced industry and technology. But the question of historical background and unique cultural tradition is, of course, posed from the very beginning. In some of his most perceptive pages, Dr Aziz separates from the chances and changes of local historical experience the fundamental principles which probably are necessary to secure any really successful development in any country that is still about three-quarters rural with perhaps 25 per cent of the country people without any land at all. But how these principles are applied in concrete national circumstances must depend upon local historical and cultural conditions and how well or ill variants, modifications, first steps and detours are taken when history and tradition appear to block the way.

But Dr Aziz has much too much wisdom and experience to deny that in some, usually encrustedly feudal, societies, none of the basic principles can be adopted because leadership lies with those from whom their application would demand the sacrifice of *not* racing on towards high industry, high technology and high Western consumerism, leaving the great majority behind. For those countries, the outcome will probably be that of Nationalist China. Only perhaps when 75 per cent of the people are up to their necks in water will the various possible adaptations of China's early rural revolution be applied. Meanwhile, Dr Aziz has written an absorbing guide for governments ready to rethink their rural priorities and a prophetic book for those who are not.

Introduction

The Third World has reached a turning point in its long and arduous struggle for economic and social development. In recent years, many Third World countries have come to realise that the development strategies they had pursued in the past two decades were inappropriate and even irrelevant to their real needs. They have also come to realise that a development strategy tied primarily to economic growth will not by itself solve problems of employment and income distribution or improve the conditions of the poorest segments of the population. Indeed, in many countries, rapid economic growth has further aggravated the problems of poverty, unemployment and inequality.

The search for alternative development strategies has now become intense, particularly among political leaders and social scientists within the Third World. The starting point for this search is the recognition that a development strategy that aims at creating a consumer society on the Western model is neither feasible nor desirable. With limited natural resources and continuous erosion of man's environment, even most of the Western countries could not sustain the present rates or patterns of growth and consumption for more than thirty or forty years. The developing countries, with such a huge backlog of poverty and with their populations threatening to double every twenty-five or thirty years, could not conceivably provide a car and a refrigerator to every family in the foreseeable future. The main focus of their development efforts, it is now widely accepted, must be on meeting the basic human needs of the entire population, rather than on providing Western levels of consumption to a privileged minority.

Conceptually, the acceptance of a basic needs approach to development can be regarded as something of a breakthrough but that by itself does not provide a practical development strategy and a set of workable policies. Many difficult political, economic and moral issues must be resolved before a development strategy based on basic needs can be evolved. The fulfilment of basic needs requires not only a rapid increase in the production of certain types of goods and services, but also a redistribution of land and other productive assets and that cannot be achieved without drastic changes in the political power structures. Once the physiological needs of the bulk of the population for food, clothing or shelter are satisfied, many supplementary needs or goals arise – for cultural growth through education and community life, for creativity and dignity through job satisfaction and a greater sense of participation, and for freedom of mobility, association or expression. How can these basic and supplementary needs be fitted into or reconciled with varying and often conflicting value systems such as personal versus collective rewards, freedom versus equality, autonomy versus solidarity? And should there be a social maximum or ceiling on personal consumption as an essential prerequisite for attaining a social minimum for everyone?

The answers to these questions would vary widely, but they seem to cluster around three different viewpoints. The supporters of a free enterprise system, with primary reliance on private ownership of the means of production, would emphasise economic objectives like higher production, more investment, larger exports and price stability. By creating incentives for maximum individual growth and a favourable climate for private investment, they would argue, rapid progress can be achieved which will trickle down in due course to the lowest income groups through fuller employment and better social services, supported by selective fiscal devices to improve income distribution. But, in practice, this has not generally happened. Even in countries which have achieved rapid economic progress, the poverty of the poorest segments of the population has remained largely undiminished, and the problems of employment and maldistribution of incomes have become more severe in most developing countries. Hollis Chenery in his Introduction to *Redistribution with Growth*, a Joint Study[1] by the World Bank and the Institute of Development Studies, has summed up this situation in the following words:

It is now clear that more than a decade of rapid growth in under-developed countries has been of little or no benefit to perhaps a third of their population. Although the average per capita income of the Third World has increased by 50 per cent since 1960, this growth has been very unequally distributed among countries, regions within countries, and socio-economic groups. Paradoxically, while growth policies have succeeded beyond the expectations of the first development decade, the very idea of aggregate growth as a social objective has increasingly been called into question.

Recent evidence confirms earlier speculations that in the early stages of development the distribution of income tends to become more concentrated. Increases in output come dispro-portionately from relatively small modern sectors of primary production and industry, which absorb a high proportion of total investment and have relatively high rates of productivity growth. This pattern of concentrated growth is perpetuated by limited access to land, credit, education, and modern-sector employment, and is often reinforced, unintentionally or otherwise, by the government's fiscal and trade policies as well as the distribution of public expenditures.

This study also shows that most of the developing countries have much greater relative inequality than the developed or the socialist countries. In half of these countries, the income share for the lowest 40 per cent of the households avereages 12 per cent; in half the countries this share is only 9 per cent.

At the other end of the scale is the socialist model in which the primary emphasis is on equality of opportunity and collective or State ownership of the means of production. Countries which have adopted such systems have in general achieved, along with rapid economic progress, a more equitable distribution of income and have thereby managed to satisfy the basic needs of the population and minimised luxury consumption and waste of resources. But the system has often involved restrictions on individual freedom and on the freedom of mobility, occupation or association. Apart from this inherent conflict between the objectives of freedom and equality, the problems of adjustment have been more difficult in some countries after the initial stages of development, with growing demand for housing, cars and other consumer goods and a gradual weakening of the initial ideological fervour.

In between these two approaches are several different mixtures which have been suggested or tried. In some, the primary reliance has remained on private ownership but policies for redistribution, employment and social justice are actively pursued. In others, the approach to economic institutions and management is basically socialistic but is blended with some political and institutional innovations which permit semi-socialist ownership, some scope for private initiative or ownership and greater freedom of mobility and occupation.

In practice, these development models and their numerous variations have produced mixed results in the past three decades. Some have been more successful than others but, as yet, there is no model or pattern which could provide the basis for at least an intellectual or academic consensus in the debate on development alternatives. This is partly because there are no agreed criteria to determine development objectives or to assess results and partly because most of the practical examples have not lived up to their theoretical or conceptual vision or offered what could be regarded as the best possible combination of political, social and economic objectives of development.

But now, in my view, at least one outstanding example of success is emerging – that of China, which deserves the most careful and sincere attention and study in our search for more meaningful development alternatives. In the 1950s and 1960s, China's success in maintaining political stability, in creating an egalitarian society and in initiating a workable economic system was widely accepted, but few outside scholars and observers were impressed with China's technological or economic results or were sure about the place and role of the individual in China. In the 1970s, when China began to open its doors to a larger number of visitors, more conclusive evidence has accumulated on China's economic and technological progress and the basic humanistic nature of China's institutions with focus on man himself. There will always be those who will persist in their doubts or those who will question one aspect or another. But in a historical perspective, China's political, social and economic progress has been truly phenomenal.

China has only 8 per cent of the world's cultivable land but 20 per cent of the world's population. And yet it has managed, without any significant external assistance, to provide adequate food for its 800 million people and meet their other basic needs of clothing, housing, medicine and education. In economic terms, it has maintained between 1952 and 1974, an average growth of over 6 per cent in gross domestic product, 3.2 per cent in agriculture and 9.7 per cent in industry. It has succeeded in eliminating absolute poverty and solving the problems of unemployment and inflation – the three most serious problems facing almost all developing countries.

In terms of social and political objectives, China has gone far beyond the narrow concept of social justice; it has created a society which provides a sense of dignity, the spirit of self-reliance and the opportunity of participation and decision-making. Above all, it has brought about a fundamental change in values and objectives of development, with greater emphasis on collective rather than individual rewards and on social rather than purely materialistic or technological objectives. Material incentives are present and important, but they are secondary and subservient to social and political objectives. These achievements were not without cost, pitfalls and mistakes but, for such a large country as China, the achievements of the past 27 years speak for themselves.

It is therefore important for other developing countries to analyse the Chinese development experience without the geopolitical prejudices and overtones that have dominated past debates about alternative development strategies and without prejudging its relevance or feasibility for other countries.

This book attempts to make a modest contribution to the current debate on development alternatives by presenting a brief assessment of the Chinese approach to *rural development*. It is not an academic treatise which tests and verifies all the quantitative data concerning the Chinese economy, nor does it present a comprehensive view of China's agricultural and rural development. It concentrates on those aspects of rural development in China which would help to determine the relevance of China's experience for other developing countries.

The first part of the book, consisting of five chapters, contains a summary review of rural development in China. The historical perspective of China's agriculture is presented in Chapter 1, and the social transformation of the rural society through various stages of collectivisation in Chapter 2. The next chapter explains the main elements of China's agricultural strategy and the results of the efforts so far made to achieve the technical transformation of China's agriculture. Chapter 4 explains the structure and organisation of the People's Communes and the gradual transition from agricultural to rural development. Chapter 5 sums up the main achievements of China in agriculture and rural development and attempts to look into China's problems and its future prospects. The first draft of this book was completed on 3 September 1976, only six days before the death of Chairman Mao Tse-tung. A postscript on 'China after Mao' has been added at the end of Chapter 5.

In many ways, Part I of this book is a self-contained evaluation of China's experience in rural development. Those who only wish to understand the Chinese approach to rural development, either as an academic exercise or to draw their own lessons from it, might wish to stop at the end of Part I. But my purpose in writing this book was not only to present my own understanding of the Chinese approach but to explore its relevance for other developing countries in the light of the following questions:

What are the unique and not so unique features of the Chinese experience?

Does the Chinese experience throw up some basic principles or factors in rural development which are fundamental to our understanding of the problems of rural development?

What are the essential prerequisites for adopting the Chinese approach in other countries and what are the main obstacles which prevent the adoption of more meaningful approaches?

Are there any intermediate approaches in which the Chinese model can be applied in stages?

Are there any partial solutions aimed at only some of the objectives of rural development?

I have attempted to answer these questions in Part II of the book by presenting in Chapter 6, five key elements of a theoretical framework for rural development. It is my contention that any rural development strategy that does not cover all the five elements cannot be successful in eliminating rural poverty or meeting the basic needs of the entire rural population. The next chapter identifies certain essential prerequisites to explore for each of the five elements of the proposed model, *inter alia*, if the essential features of the Chinese approach can be pursued under political and cultural circumstances that may be different from those of China.

All social sciences must deal with imperfect situations if all the prerequisites for the perfect solution cannot be met. To contend with the realities of our imperfect world, Chapter 8 discusses the need for intermediate or partial solutions to problems of rural poverty. Even in countries where drastic political changes necessary for the adoption of the comprehensive model of rural development are not feasible in the short run, certain intermediate solutions could, by gradually increasing the incomes of the poorest segments of the population and their weight in the political power structure, prepare the ground for comprehensive solutions in future. Partial solutions, on the other hand, while improving the lot of the poor in absolute terms, cannot improve the overall pattern of income distribution or the nature of social and political relationships in the society, and cannot therefore lead to rural development in any meaningful sense.

The concluding chapter again emphasises the main lessons of the Chinese experience and their success in taking a unified view of political, social and economic objectives.

The book is essentially written for the political leader and the policymaker in developing countries, particularly those who are looking for more meaningful development strategies. Even if only a few of them find the analysis and main conclusions relevant to this search, my purpose in writing this book will have been more than fulfilled.

SARTAJ AZIZ

Rome, March 1977

Part I

RURAL DEVELOPMENT IN CHINA

'WALKING ON TWO LEGS'

The Historical Perspective

The history of agriculture in China is at least 4500 years old. As early as 2500 B.C. the central plain of northern China was supporting a sizeable rural population, growing millet and later rice brought in from south-east Asia and wheat brought in from Eurasia. By 1500 B.C. the inhabitants were using bronze; the Iron Age revolution took place between 700 and 600 B.C. The rise and fall of various dynasties which ruled China from one century to the other, were accompanied by massive movement of peasants into newly conquered lands and the building of large irrigation works. As Joseph Needham points out: 'The importance of irrigation channels for intensive agriculture, water conservancy for preventing floods and canal transport for gathering in of tribute to the Imperial Court from the Provinces, led to the establishment of a veritable tradition of great public works, which is absolutely living in China today, as much as it ever was in the Han, Ch'in or Tiang dynasties.[1]

According to the best available estimates,[2] the population of China was about 65 million in the year A.D. 1400 and the total cultivated area about 24–28 million hectares or less than half a hectare per person. The population of China is estimated to have increased to about 200 million by 1750, to 410 million by 1850 and to 583 million in the official census year of 1953. This was an almost tenfold increase in five and a half centuries, or an annual increase of 0.4 per cent per annum. The increase was not, however, sustained or continuous and was interrupted at least twice. In the seventeenth century, the Chinese population was estimated to have fallen in absolute terms by about 20 per cent – from 150–160 million to 120–125 million – following the downfall of the Ming and the advent of the Manchus. The second decline was more severe and occurred during the Taiping rebellion of 1860 – 4. While in China's history there were long spells of peace and progress in which new lands were opened, by the middle of the nineteenth century most of the cultivable land had been colonised. The increasing pressure of population on land and the feudal nature of land holding led to many upheavals, the most serious being the Taiping Rebellion which ·cost about 20 – 30 million lives. Because of the brutal manslaughter and the disruption of life which continued after the rebellion, the population of China is estimated to have declined from 410 million in 1850 to 350 million in 1873, recovering to 430 million only in 1913.

The cultivated land of China also increased steadily from 24–28 million hectares in 1400 to 50 million by 1685, to 83 million in 1893 and to 120 million in 1936, but declined to 98 million in 1949. The total increase in area over these five and a half centuries was thus four times against a ten-fold increase in population.

The most striking feature of Chinese agriculture is the relative scarcity of cultivable land. Despite the colonisation and reclamation of additional lands over the centuries, only 15 to 20 per cent of China's land surface of 960 million hectares (9.6 million square kilometres or 3.7 million square miles) is cultivable. By 1949 only 10.2 per cent (98 million hectares) was cultivated, largely in river valleys of south and central China and in the north-eastern part of the country. About 90 per cent of China's population lives in one-sixth of the area. In the middle and lower valley of the Yangtse and the Red Basin of Szechwan, population densities range from 500 to 600 per square kilometre. The total arable land for each person living in the rural areas in China (0.25 hectares per person) is, in fact, one of the lowest in the world (see Appendix A).

Another important feature of China's agriculture is its vulnerability to natural calamities and the extreme diversity of growing conditions. For centuries the Chinese farmer has lived precariously under the constant threat of climatic uncertainty. In the humid south, he was constantly threatened by floods; while in the semi-arid north and north-west, the recurrent drought was a persistent enemy. Many regions, like East China, suffered from both.

Grain production in China in 1400 is estimated at 20 million tons, some 75 million tons in 1770 and 130 million tons in the mid-1940s. Since the total increase in grain production over this period was six and a half times, against a four-fold increase in cultivated area, it is easy to see that only about 60 per cent of the increase in grain production was obtained from larger acreage. The remainder came from increased productivity. This increase was achieved partly because of an expanding labour force, but also by more irrigation, double cropping and use of improved seed and organic manures. The Chinese were experimenting with new rice seeds even in the fifteenth century. In the sixteenth century, following the European discovery of America, the cultivation of corn and potatoes was introduced in China, and this led to important changes in the cropping patterns of some provinces.

In historical terms, this advance in agricultural techniques was a remarkable achievement and enabled China to support, despite unavoidable year-to-year fluctuations, a growing population at least until the middle of the nineteenth century. That period, coinciding with the Taiping Rebellion, marks the real beginning of China's poverty, which reached its gruesome climax by the beginning of the twentieth century. In 1911, the Nationalist movement, led by Sun Yat-Sen, overthrew the Manchu Empire and set up the Republic of China, but the new regime never fulfilled its promise to give the peasants their 'equalisation rights'. The traditional pattern of land-holding continued, and the Chinese capitalists and some outside interests also joined hands with landlord groups to ravage the country. In the next twenty years, administrative corruption and incompetence increased enormously, the disruption caused by the civil war and then the Japanese invasion created many new and serious problems and all these factors plunged the Chinese masses into a nightmare existence of hunger and impoverishment. The largest famine in man's history occurred in China in 1928–9 when between 3 and 6 million people died of starvation in Northern China alone.

The number of dead in this period are not cold statistics, but the suffering of a living people with a great past. The depth and agony of this suffering can be gleaned only from the first-hand accounts of many who survived. Jan Myrdal in his *Report from a Chinese Village* records the following memory of Fu Hai-tsao.[3]

'We came to Yenan from Hengshan when I was five. That was during the great famine of 1928. We had been thrown out. My father brought the family with him here. Father starved to death the next year. We went about begging in 1929. We had nothing to eat. Father went to Chaochuan to gather firewood and beg food but he didn't get any. He was carrying elm leaves and firewood when he fell by the roadside. He was lying on his face and was dead. The elm leaves and firewood were still there beside him. No one had touched a thing. The elm leaves were for us to eat. He wasn't ill; he had just starved to death. Mother says that he used to be big and strong and had been a good worker, thoughtful and kind to the family and open-handed if anyone was ill. That is my earliest memory: of always being hungry, and of Father lying there dead in the road.' (Fu Hai-tsao.)

William Hinton in his book *Fanshen* records the story of Wang Ch'ung-lai's wife who was bought as a wife at the age of nine for nine copper coins (one silver Chinese dollar) by the landlord's widow for her servant to secure another servant in the house:[4]

After six years we saved enough to buy an acre of land. Then came the famine year. Ch'ung-lai had to come home from Taiyuan but he was sick. From the land we got two bags of grain. After paying the tax there was nothing left. Hunger made Ch'ung-lai sicker. By that time I had two children, a boy and a girl. We three went out to beg. Sometimes we had to go very far away and couldn't find a temple to stay in and had to sleep outdoors. Once I asked the children, 'Are you frightened?' They said, 'We are not afraid as long as we can find something to eat.'

But because it was a famine year it was very hard to find food. We had to sell the land. We got six bushels of millet and lived a whole year on it. We added whatever we could find to go with it. But it was hard to find anything. There weren't even any leaves left on the trees.

'In the old China,' the Chinese repeatedly tell their visitors, 'there were three big mountains on the back of the people – imperialism, feudalism and bureaucratic capitalism, with marked class differentiation in the rural areas. The poor and small peasants who accounted for over 70 per cent of the population, owned only 10 per cent of the land, and the landlords and rich peasants, with only 10 per cent of the population, owned two-thirds of all cultivable land. The peasants had to pay exorbitant land rents, heavy duties and taxes at high interest rates. These were the three knives in the peasants' back. Productivity was very low and the average yield for food grains was only 1 ton per hectare. As a result, China had to import food grains and cotton in spite of its rich land resources and favourable growing conditions.'[5]

The impact of China's geography and history on the life of the Chinese masses is vivid and cruel. Confronted with adverse natural conditions and a growing pressure of population, the Chinese peasant struggled hard and acquired valuable experience of large-scale public works for controlling floods and building irrigation channels. He also began to experiment with new agricultural techniques, better seeds and improved fertilizers long before farmers in other parts of the world knew much about improving agriculture. But despite this rich heritage of hard work and improved agriculture, the rural masses of China began to slide into chronic poverty in the nineteenth century. Man's vulnerability to natural calamities and to disease is not unrelated to his capacity to control his environment. If he is given the opportunity to organise himself to control the rivers that flood his land or to store water for use in a drought and to develop and share technology and knowledge to fight disease and hunger, he can bring about a profound change in his relationship with nature and that change in turn can prepare him for further progress. But such an opportunity was denied to the Chinese peasant by the traditional land-holding structure, in which landlords and rich peasants owned the bulk of the cultivable land and the poor peasant often did not get even the means of survival for his exacting labour.[6]

The Chinese Revolution culminating in 1949, gave the Chinese peasant this opportunity to change his relationship with nature and his future. He has shown what can be accomplished in a single generation.

2

The Social Transformation
of Rural China

The social transformation of a rural society in a developing country involves many complex socio-political issues. The first, and often the most obvious problem, is the pattern of landholding. If, a small group of landlords own and control a considerable proportion of total land and a majority of the rural population consists of small farmers, tenants or landless workers, the majority will have little hope of any improvement in their life until they obtain a fair share of the land through land reforms.

But the second and in a sense a more important aspect of rural transformation is the nature of social relationships. Land reforms can impose a ceiling on larger holdings and redistribute land to poor tenants or landless workers, but they may not by themselves change the social relationship between the medium landlords who are below the prescribed ceiling and their tenants, and the resumed land may be a very small proportion of the total land, with limited benefits for a small proportion of the tenants and landless workers. The social transformation of a rural society can begin only when the land reforms are drastic enough, not only in achieving a more equitable distribution of all the available land but in changing the nature of social relationship in a manner that will eliminate or minimise exploitation and create greater equality based on egalitarian ethics.

The third crucial aspect of social transformation is a more positive one. Even after land has been redistributed and the negative features of the old system reflected in inequitable relationships have been changed, there will be a need for a new relationship in which the new landholders can work together to improve their land and water resources, increase their production and incomes and organise a dynamic, rural community.

This is seldom smooth and easy. Initially, rural society in a poor, developing country is like a pyramid with landlords and high officials at the top and the poor masses at the bottom. If, through a violent revolution or even a gradual, peaceful social change, political power can be transferred to the poor majority, the pyramid is turned upside down, with a tremendous weight on what was previously the pinnacle. The task of converting this inverted pyramid into a circle by gradually rounding off the corners and building new and harmonious relationships is one of the most complicated political problems known to man.

In China the revolutionary struggle of the Communist Party began in the 1920s as a reaction to the prevailing agrarian situation. In his famous study prepared in 1926, 'Analysis of Classes in Chinese Society', Mao Tse-tung discussed the potential of the various classes to wage struggle to secure their rights. In 1927, he completed another study entitled 'Investigation of the Peasant Movement in Hunan', which emphasised the key role of poor peasants in the revolution, while carefully analysing the power structure of other groups in rural society. In subsequent years, as certain areas were liberated, land and property belonging to landlords were redistributed on an equal basis, with the landlords and rich peasants retaining an equal share.

The total liquidation of the traditional system of land ownership and social stratification could not, however, be completed until the establishment of the People's Republic of China in 1949. In 1947, a draft Agrarian Law was passed to proclaim 'the end of feudal and semi-feudal exploitation and the realisation of the system of land to the tiller'. But the implementation of the policy took about three years, from 1949 to 1952, and required establishment of peasant associations in all parts of the country and mass meetings to educate and mobilise the peasants against the landlords and rich peasants. The criteria[1] for classifying the rural population into landlords, rich peasants, middle peasants and poor peasants, was an important feature of the Agrarian Law of 1947. A *landlord* was a person owning a lot of land and deriving his entire income from rents collected from peasants without any participation in manual work. *Rich peasants* also owned a good piece of land and all the farm implements needed. Unlike the landlords they did participate in manual work but a part of their income was secured through exploitation since they sub-let a part of their land, or the land taken from landlords, to poor peasants. *Middle peasants* had their own land and implements; they neither sold their own labour nor hired other peasants. *Poor peasants* on the other hand had no land or very little land and some tools, and supplemented their meagre income by working on the land owned by landlords or rich peasants. *Tenant farmers* were those members of the rural population who had neither land nor tools and survived by selling their labour at very low wages. In many cases, the past behaviour and attitude of landlords and rich peasants was given greater importance than the actual size of their land-holding. Once the classification was completed, the party leaders, supported by students and teachers from urban areas, were supposed to encourage the middle and poor peasants to seize the lands and property of the landlords. It is difficult to assess the number of landlords who were physically eliminated;[2] but a very large proportion of landlords and rich peasants were 'reformed' and 'absorbed' in the new structure.[3]

The next step was to redistribute the land and property among the poor and middle peasants, including the landlords and rich peasants who were prepared to 'reform' themselves and live on allotted holdings. According to official figures, about 46.6 million hectares of land was distributed among 300 million landless and land-poor peasants, each receiving an average of 0.15 hectares.[4]

By 1952, a complete reform of the agrarian system had been carried out, but the production pattern in the village was still fundamentally unchanged. The reforms did, however, destroy the traditional agrarian structure and created favourable conditions for further steps in the transformation of China's rural society.

China's transition from a small peasant economy towards a collective agriculture is usually divided into four stages:

    (i) Mutual aid teams.
   (ii) Elementary co-operatives.
  (iii) Advanced co-operatives.
  (iv) People's communes.

These stages were traversed in a short period of six years, between 1952 and 1958, and there was some overlap between (ii) and (iii). The important distinction does not therefore lie in the temporal sequence of these stages but in the nature of the social change effected by each stage in China's agrarian structure and in the degree of collectivisation achieved. This period also coincided with China's first Five Year Plan (1953–7).

MUTUAL AID TEAMS

The *first* step towards collectivisation was the formation of mutual aid teams. After the land reforms in 1946–9, the initial efforts of the Chinese peasants to increase production ran into difficulties because of the relative scarcity of means of production. Some peasants had somewhat larger plots of land but not enough animals or farm implements; others had more animals than they could use on their own plots of land. By grouping six, eight or ten households into mutual aid teams, peasants could pool, as they had done to some extent in the past, their labour, animals and farm implements, while retaining individual ownership of the land. The value of a man's labour or the work done by a member's draught animal was determined through an agreed local standard. Some teams were seasonal, others were permanent. By the end of 1952, 40 per cent of China's rural households had organised themselves into 8 million 'permanent' and seasonal mutual aid teams.

The grouping of small peasants into mutual aid teams facilitated the initial task of utilising available means of production more effectively, but the capacity of these teams for sustained progress was limited. They could not cope with national disasters, undertake larger projects, purchase agricultural machinery or use more advanced techniques. Many of the teams also encountered contradictions arising from efforts to combine individual ownership of land and means of production with collective work on the land. There was a natural desire for each member to complete work on his own field first. Some peasants, unable to cope with disasters, sold their land to other peasants and hired themselves out to more prosperous peasants.

ELEMENTARY CO-OPERATIVES

To overcome the limitations of the mutual aid teams, the second stage of collectivisation, in the form of elementary or semi-socialist Agricultural Producers' Co-operatives, was initiated in 1953. Simple credit or marketing co-operatives had been set up even before 1953 to replace the middle man, but the big step was to set up producers' co-operatives in which land could be pooled for joint or collective cultivation. The main characteristic of these elementary co-operatives was their recognition of the system of individual property rights in the system of income distribution. About 60 to 70 per cent of the total income was distributed on the basis of the work done by each member of the co-operative, but 30 to 40 per cent of the income was distributed as dividends or rent for land or other means of production contributed by various members, which constituted the share capital of the co-operative. Membership in the co-operatives was voluntary, and it was possible for members to terminate their membership and withdraw their land. Management of the co-operative was the responsibility of a committee elected each year by all the members. By 1955, about one third of peasant households had formed about 633,000 elementary producers' co-operatives.

ADVANCED CO-OPERATIVES

The third stage in China's rural development was that of advanced producers' co-operatives. In many ways, this stage was more significant than the second, because in an advanced co-operative, the entire income of the co-operative was distributed among members on the basis of the work done for the co-operative and not on the basis of the land or implements contributed by members. The advanced co-operatives were also much larger in size and were formed by amalgamating ten, fifteen or twenty elementary co-operatives. In practice, the typical advanced co-operatives covered one natural village – with a population ranging from 1000 to 3000 and a cultivable area ranging from 300 to 800 hectares. They had therefore much larger capital with which to acquire agricultural machinery, undertake large irrigation and flood-control projects and finance small-scale rural industries.

The most important prerequisite for the success of elementary and the advanced producers' co-operatives in China was the equal distribution of land after the revolution. Since 1949, most families in China had less than a quarter hectare of land and the total income from this land was not very much more than the potential wage that could be earned by all the members of the family. The formation of producers' co-operatives, in which the bulk of the income was allotted on the basis of the work done, did not thus adversely affect their incomes. The position would be radically different if there were some holdings of say 10, 5 or even 2 hectares. The total income from such holdings would be larger than the sum total of wages earned by the members of the family, and their owners would naturally be reluctant to pool their land, farm animals or implements in a producers' co-operative.

The second prerequisite was, of course, directly related to the results achieved by collectivisation. If production and incomes expand as a result of collectivisation, then there is greater enthusiasm for co-operatives and the next steps become easier. In China, this was achieved with active support from the Government at different levels. Initially, the Hsiang, which was the lowest unit of local administration, gave loans to those poor and middle peasants who could not afford to pay their share capital to become members of the co-operatives. In October 1955, the Sixth Plenary Session of the Seventh Central Committee of the Chinese Communist Party adopted certain important 'Decisions on Agricultural Co-operation' and asked various departments and banks to increase their financial assistance to co-operatives for mechanisation, irrigation and capital works. The Hsiang administration were directed to provide technical know-how in agriculture and trained personnel for the co-operatives. Assistance was also provided in the planning and construction of local industries.

The results of these efforts were on the whole very positive, and harvests in 1955 and 1956 were visibly better, although in 1957 crops were poor. By the end of 1956 some 88 per cent and by the summer of 1957 almost 97 per cent of the total peasant population had been organised into 740,000 advanced co-operatives.

Despite this rapid pace of collectivisation between 1953 and 1957, the transition was not without difficulties. There were some middle peasants who had a larger supply of farm implements and felt better off on their own piece of land. There were others in more remote villages who had acquired local leadership and could see prospects of enlarging their holding by buying up the land of the poor peasants. These elements began to advocate a slower and more flexible approach to collectivisation. Some peasants also began to talk of the right 'to select partners' in a co-operative.

This kind of tendency could not be countered only by financial or technical assistance to co-operatives or by larger harvests. They had to be met by a powerful political and organisational movement to prevent the 'return of capitalism'. The efforts to organise co-operatives was therefore accompanied by a mass political campaign. Special movements were launched against corruption, waste and bureaucracy and against the 'five evils of capitalists', namely bribery of Government workers, tax evasion, theft of State property, cheating on Government contracts and stealing economic information for private speculation. Adult education was organised on a large scale, party cadres and local administrators were mobilised to tour the countryside extensively and promote greater political consciousness among the peasants. They also explained the advantages of collectivisation and the dangers created by continued concern for private ownership. In this campaign they naturally presented examples of early successes achieved by co-operatives and encouraged others to join hands in order to undertake bigger projects to develop their land and water resources.

THE PEOPLE'S COMMUNES

It was this combination of results achieved by the co-operatives and the success of the political movement to mobilise support for collectivisation that prepared the ground for the next and fourth stage of collectivisation – *The People's Communes*. While the advanced co-operatives had achieved the important step of moving from private to collective or communal ownership of land, they were still too small in size to undertake larger irrigation schemes or build many industrial units. At the same time, there was the need to create a unit of rural development that could go beyond agriculture and manage all the economic, administrative, social and political aspects of rural life. This was achieved by merging agricultural co-operatives and the lowest administrative units (hsiang) into 'People's Communes'.

The creation of the people's communes was accompanied by another mass movement to consolidate the changes that had already taken place and to prepare the ground for further collectivisation. Chairman Mao himself toured the countryside in the summer of 1958 to evaluate the situation and lend his personal prestige to the movement. The Central Committee of the Party adopted a resolution, in August 1958, on setting up the people's communes.[5] The amalgamation of advanced co-operatives and Hsiangs into people's communes was very rapid and the process was almost complete by the end of September 1958, by which time 740,000 advanced co-operatives had been reconstituted into 26,000 communes.

The transition from semi-socialist co-operatives to fully socialist communes was much faster than even Mao himself had anticipated[6] in 1955 and was an important element of China's departure from the Soviet model of industrialisation and urbanisation. But in political and social terms the new system of communes was somewhat ahead of its time. Chinese society was not yet ready to make the transition from socialism to communism and start working on the principle of 'from each according to ability, to each according to need' (rather than 'to each according to work'). The intention to provide free food to everyone was given up fairly soon and the proposal to centralise planning and accounting functions at the commune was not followed. Production and distribution decisions were transferred back to the production brigade and more usually to the production team, which became the accounting unit and in effect the basic collective unit for actual cultivation. The new size of the commune, merging two or three old Hsiangs, also proved unwieldy and disrupted some of the old communication and administrative arrangements built around the traditional market town. The 26,000 communes were again sub-divided into 74,000 communes.[7] The system of private plots which had been absorbed into the communes was also reintroduced, but the total area to be covered by private plots was not to exceed 5 per cent of the total land under the collective as against 10 per cent before 1958. The new size of the private plot was thus much smaller and was like a back garden to enable the farmer to produce pigs, poultry and vegetables either for the use of the family or for sale at the village fairs introduced in 1960 to supplement his income.

With these changes, the Chinese managed to create a more viable institutional framework for rural development that judiciously combined the tremendous surge of socialist consciousness that had already been generated with the political reality of the time and the economic self-interest of the Chinese farmer.

The debate generated by the agricultural crisis of 1959–61 was not confined to the size of the commune and its internal working but involved a serious reappraisal of China's agrarian policy. There was by then a general consensus on much greater priority for agriculture, but there was no clear view of specific new policies that could be introduced. Some suggested decentralising the commune and, in 1961, the policy of 'three private and one guarantee' was, in fact, advocated. This implied the reintroduction of private plots, enlargement of markets for privately produced goods and larger production of handicraft goods. In return, the holder of the private plot would guarantee to produce a certain quota. Thus, in addition to restrictions on the buying and selling of land, this approach would have meant a restricted return to private farming. Another approach advocated much larger State investment in agriculture, particularly for machinery, and argued that agricultural production using machinery in a big way could not be operated in a disorganised manner and that it was beyond the power of a small peasant economy to operate modern technical equipment. There was some opposition to this latter approach since it meant diverting resources from industry to agriculture.

These different lines of argument were finally resolved in September 1962 at the Tenth Plenary Session of the Eighth Central Committee of the Chinese Communist Party which decided to accord high priority to agriculture. The relevant portion of the communique on this subject is reproduced below:

> It is necessary to mobilize and concentrate the strength of the whole Party and the whole nation in an active way to give agriculture and the collective economy of the People's Communes every possible material, technical and financial aid as well as aid in the field of leadership and personnel, and to bring about the technical transformation of agriculture, stage by stage in a manner suited to local conditions . . . the urgent task facing the people of our country at present is to carry through

the general policy of developing the national economy, with agriculture as the foundation and industry the leading factor . . .[8]

This new policy led to the now famous slogan 'take agriculture as the foundation and industry as the leading factor'. The success of China in presenting important elements of their strategy or policy in simple slogans, which can be grasped at all levels, has been remarkable. In fact, the evolution of China's agricultural strategy can be gleaned from successive slogans presented and adopted from time to time. These slogans not only increase understanding of policies at lower levels but add a certain ideological strength to their implementation. Cadres and workers are more willing to follow a certain technique or policy for ideological reasons even if its economic benefits have not yet been demonstrated.

The decision of the Tenth Plenary Session to shift emphasis to technical transformation was a landmark in China's agriculture, but it did not mean the relegation of the social aspect. The same session also decided 'never forget class struggle'. A Socialist Education Movement[9] was launched in 1962 to recreate enthusiasm for socialist agriculture despite the setbacks of the preceding three years, although its other aims included a cleaning-up of rural cadres and a revival of the class struggle in the light of the behaviour and performance of different individuals during the difficult years.

Notwithstanding the setbacks of 1959–61 and the subsequent adjustments in the commune system, the system met this initial challenge successfully. The Chinese were not unfamiliar with natural calamities, but for the first time they were organised enough to meet them. They worked together to provide relief, to build embankments and water wells. There was austerity but everyone shared it. The concern of the Government for the well-being of the masses was equally visible. As a result, even those who were hesitant supporters of collective agriculture began to recognise the importance of organised effort to meet calamities and to improve the life of the rural community.

The manner in which the people's communes function and their contribution to rural development in China for the next two decades is discussed in greater detail in Chapter 4.

3

The Technical Transformation of Agriculture

China's long and continuous record of agricultural progress has been mentioned in Chapter 1. Over the centuries the Chinese not only acquired valuable experience in colonising, reclaiming and irrigating new land, but also learnt how to increase productivity, through the use of better seeds and organic manures. In a technological sense and in comparison with most other countries of Asia or Africa, China's agriculture at the time of liberation in 1949 was relatively advanced, with grain yields ranging from less than 1 ton in north-east China to 3 tons per hectare in southern China. But by the middle of the nineteenth century all the area that could be reclaimed and irrigated through the traditional gravity system had been brought under cultivation and efforts to increase yields with the technology known at that time through improved seeds and more organic manure had virtually reached their ceiling. As population pressure continued to increase, without a corresponding increase in area or yields, the balance between food and population and between effort and reward began to crumble, causing widespread suffering and deprivation among a growing segment of the population. The intensity of this suffering was further aggravated by the traditional system of land-holding. The efforts of the landlords to extract the maximum possible surplus from the peasant not only exposed him to perpetual hunger but also destroyed his capacity and his motivation to improve his land.

In this situation, the prospects of further progress in the agricultural sector depended initially on the liquidation of the feudal system to give the peasant a fair chance to secure the means of survival and a fair return for his labours and to help him regain the motivation and the capacity to improve his land. But after that further progress called for a sustained improvement in agricultural technology and for the availability of modern inputs. At lower levels of agricultural technology, it is possible for agricultural production to grow at least at the same rate as the input of labour for a considerable period of time, but there is a limit to what a rural labour force can accomplish, without improved technology, adequate education and training and modern inputs like chemical fertiliser and machinery.

In the first ten years between 1949 and 1958, when a basic structural change in the rural society was being undertaken, the agricultural strategy in China was aimed at organising and maximising the use of traditional resources, mainly labour and organic manures. Repairs of the pre-war irrigation systems were undertaken and labour-intensive water-conservancy projects were undertaken. As a result, the production of grain, which is a good index of China's agricultural progress, increased from 108 million tons in 1949 to 154 million tons in 1952 and 205 million tons in 1958, but dropped to a range of 150–70 million tons between 1959 and 1961. It recovered to 200 million tons again only in 1965, and then increased steadily to 240 million tons in 1970 and 275 million tons in 1974, as shown in Table 3.1 on page 20. Apart from very adverse weather conditions in the period 1959–61, there is no doubt that over-emphasis on intensive cultivation through close planting and more irrigation, without adequate drainage and a corresponding increase in fertiliser and farm machinery, did not lead to satisfactory results, particularly in areas in which productivity was already relatively high. China's own production of chemical fertilisers in 1949 was only 27,000 tons and increased very little in the next few years.

While recognising the importance of improved technology and modern inputs, the Chinese leaders assigned first priority to the social transformation of agriculture, partly to ensure that the benefits of technical change were distributed equally and did not recreate a privileged class, and partly to organise the rural community in such a way as to acquire, disseminate and finance the improved technology and modern inputs largely through their own efforts. The manner in which these different stages of the social and technical transformation were to be interwoven and the relationship between agriculture and industry also

Table 3.1 Grain Production 1949–75

Year	Output (Mill. Metric Ton)	Increase (%)
1949	108	–
1950	125	15.7
1951	135	8.0
1952	154	14.1
1953	157	1.9
1954	160	1.9
1955	175	9.4
1956	183	4.6
1957	185	1.1
1958	(205)	10.8
1959	(170)	−17.0
1960	150	−11.7
1961	(160)	6.7
1962	170	6.3
1963	(182)	7.1
1964	(195)	7.1
1965	200	2.6
1966	(220)	10.0
1967	230	4.5
1968	(234)	1.7
1969	(237)	1.3
1970	240	1.3
1971	246	2.5
1972	240	− 2.4
1973	250	4.2
1974	275	10.0
1975	(285)	3.6

NOTE: All figures in brackets in the table are *estimates*.

Sources:

1949–57	*Ten Great Years*, op. cit. p. 119.
1958–9	Estimate by Chao, op. cit. p. 246.
1960	A statement of Mao Tse-tung to Viscount Montgomery, *The Times* (London, 15 October 1961), cited in Chao, op. cit. p. 245.
1961, 1963	Estimates by Chao, op. cit. p. 245.
1962	Given by Chou En-lai to a Pakistani reporter. See 'Dawn' (Karachi, 11 April 1963), cited in Chao, op. cit. p. 245.
1964	'Output close to 200 million tons'. Given by Chou En-lai to Edgar Snow, see 'Asahi' (Tokyo, 27 February 1965), cited

	in Chao, op. cit. p. 245.
1965	'Chinese News Summary', 28 April 1966. Cited in Chao, op. cit. p. 245.
1966	Han Suyin, *China in the Year 2001* (New York: Basic Books, 1967) p. 54. Cited in Stavis, op. cit. p. 13.
1967	A. L. Strong, *Letter from China*, 1 January 1968, cited in Stavis, op. cit. p. 13. The estimates for 1966 and 1967 are fairly consistent with those made by the Chinese before the end of 1967. (See Stavis p. 13 for details.)
1968–9	Estimates by Stavis intermediate between 1967 and 1970.
1970	Edgar Snow, 'Talks with Chou En-lai: The Open Door', *New Republic*, Vol. 164, No. 13, 27 March 1971, p. 20, cited in Stavis, op. cit. p. 13.
1971	*Peking Review*, No. 2, 14 January 1972, p. 7.
1972	*Peking Review*, No. 1, 5 January 1973, p. 12.
1973	*Peking Review*, No. 1, 4 January 1974, p. 8 reported that the total grain output in 1973 outstripped that of 1971 (previously the highest on record).
1974	Agriculture and Forestry Minister Yan Li-kung told FAO on 14 November 1975 that the 1974 total grain output was 274.9 million tonnes. See *Financial Times* (London, 3 December 1975).
1975	Author's estimates.

EXPLANATORY NOTE: The question of the comparability of Chinese food-grain output figures before and after 1959 has been widely discussed. It is certain that in the beginning, i.e. before and during the First Plan, the Chinese used the earlier Soviet approach of measuring the harvest in terms of biological yield, or fruit on the stalk. Furthermore, grain figures were given in terms of Unified Grain Equivalent (U.G.E.), thus including pulses and groundnuts at a conversion rate of 2:1 and roots and tubers at a conversion rate of 4:1. This method seems to have been abandoned after 1960 or 1961. As a first step, the biological yield concept was replaced by the more conventional yield approach, net of harvesting losses. At a later stage, possibly mid-1960s, soyabeans, rape-seed and groundnuts seem to have been excluded. Furthermore, sweet potatoes seem to have been excluded while white potatoes, cassava and yams apparently are still included. But here, the conversion rate seems to have gone to 5:1. According to Audrey Donnithorne's report from her visit to China in 1974, produce from the private plots also is excluded. If present Chinese food-grain output would be expressed in terms of 1958 coverage, aggregate figures would be much higher. For example, the 1968 harvest was reported by one visitor (A. Strong, *Newsletter from China*, January 1969) to be 330 million tons U.G.E. The series of official figures given by Chinese authorities to Burki for the period 1958 to 1965–215, 192, 161, 189, 203, 219, 238, 258 million tons respectively (*China Quarterly*, No. 41, London, January 1970) seem to be based on the latest coverage and methodology now in use in China, at least from 1970 onwards when the first official estimate of 240 million was given out for total grain production.

received considerable attention in the formulation of China's approach to rural development.

POLICY GUIDELINES

As early as 1955, Chairman Mao in an article dated 31 July 1955, entitled *On the Question of Agricultural Co-operation*, recognised the importance of 'technical reform' *after* the social reform in the following words:

> During the First and Second Five-Year Plans, the main feature of reform in the countryside will still be social reform. Technical reform will take second place. The amount of sizable farm machinery will certainly have increased, but not to any great extent. During the Third Five-Year Plan, social and technical reform will advance side by side in the rural areas. More and more large farm machinery will be employed year by year. As for social reform, co-operatives after 1960 will gradually change, group by group and at different times from co-operatives of a semi-socialist nature to fully socialist ones. Only when socialist transformation of the social-economic system is complete and when, in the technical field, all branches of production and places wherein work can be done by machinery are using it, will the social and economic appearance of China be radically changed. The economic conditions of our country being what they are, technical reform will take longer than social reform. It is estimated that it will take roughly twenty to twenty-five years to accomplish, in the main, the technical reform of agriculture on a national scale. The whole Party must work to carry out this great task.[1]

In another article in 1957, *On the Correct Handling of Contradictions among the People*, Mao explained the relationship between agriculture and industry:

> In discussing our path to industrialization, I am here concerned principally with the relationship between the growth of heavy industry, light industry, and agriculture. Heavy industry is the core of China's economic construction. This must

be affirmed. But at the same time, full attention must be paid to the development of agriculture and light industry.

As China is a great agricultural country, with over eighty per cent of its population in the villages, its industry and agriculture must be developed simultaneously. Only then will industry have raw materials and a market, and only so will it be possible to accumulate fairly large funds for the building up of a powerful heavy industry. Everyone knows that light industry is closely related to agriculture. Without agriculture there can be no light industry. But it is not so clearly understood that agriculture provides heavy industry with an important market. This fact, however, will be more readily appreciated as the gradual progress of technological improvement and modernization of agriculture calls for more and more machinery, fertilizers, water conservancy and electric power projects, and transport facilities for the farms, as well as fuel and building materials for the rural consumers. The entire national economy will benefit if we can achieve an even greater growth in our agriculture and thus induce a correspondingly greater development of light industry during the period of the Second and Third Five-Year Plans. With the development of agriculture and light industry, heavy industry will be assured of its market and funds and thus grow fast faster.[2]

These pronouncements about the relationship between social and technical reforms in agriculture and between agriculture, light industry and heavy industry, made at a time when in almost all developing countries, development was synonymous with industrialisation and when development literature was concerned mainly with drawing surplus labour from the 'traditional' to the 'modern' sector, are a remarkable contribution to development policy. These general statements of policy were soon followed by efforts to spell out more clearly certain concrete and operational guidelines for agricultural development. In 1956–7, a comprehensive programme called 'The National Programme for Agricultural Development' was formulated and after extensive discussion was finally adopted by the Second Session of the Second People's Congress in April 1960. This forty-point programme established specific goals and targets for the twelve-year period from 1956 to 1967 and spelled out the measures by which they could be achieved. It called for raising annual average yields of grain crops in the three principle grain-growing areas from 150 catties per mou (1.12 tons per hectare) to 400 catties (3.0 tons per hectare) in the areas north of the Yellow River; from 208 catties (1.56 tons per hectare) to 500 catties (3.75 tons per hectare) and from 400 catties per mou (3.0 tons per hectare) to 800 per mou (6.0 tons per hectare) in areas south of Huai River. It also called for expanding irrigated land from 390 million mou (26 million hectares) in 1955 to 900 million mou (60 million hectares) in 1967; and raising production of chemical fertilizer from 0.8 million absolute tons to 15 million tons in 1967. Although some specific targets laid down in the National Programme may have been too ambitious, the Programme is still remarkable for its scope, vision and simplicity of approach.[3]

In another major document called *Sixty Work Methods*,[4] formulated in January 1958, Mao Tse-tung issued comprehensive guidelines on the political and social reorganisation of society, on planning and evaluation, on the class struggle and the role of the party cadres. Article 1 listed fourteen items of work in socialist construction which Party Committees at the *hsien* or higher level were asked to grasp:

(i) industry; (ii) handicrafts; (iii) agriculture; (iv) rural side occupations; (v) forestry; (vi) fishery; (vii) animal husbandry; (viii) communications and transport; (ix) commerce; (x) finance and banking; (xi) labor, wages and population; (xii) science; (xiii) culture and education; (xiv) public health.

Article 3 extracted fourteen items of work in socialist agriculture from the forty-point 'National Programme for Agricultural Development' and emphasised the need for greater attention to these items, while striving for all the forty points. These fourteen points were:

(i) output targets; (ii) water conservation; (iii) fertilizer; (iv) soil; (v) seed; (vi) change of systems (change of farming systems, e.g. enlargement of the multiple cropping area, change of late crop into early crop, change of early crop into

307.72   Az37r

C. 1

paddy); (vii) plant diseases and insect pests; (viii) mechanisation (modern farm implements, double-wheel, double-blade ploughs, water pumps, tractors and motor-driven means of transport); (ix) intensive cultivation; (x) animal husbandry; (xi) side occupations; (xii) afforestation; (xiii) elimination of four pests; (xiv) medical treatment and hygiene.

Article 21 on 'uninterrupted revolution' said:

Our revolutions were launched one after another. The seizure of political power on a nationwide scale in 1949 was followed by the agrarian reform against feudalism, and as soon as the agrarian reform was carried through, agricultural co-operation was initiated. This was followed by the socialist transformation of private industry and commerce and handicraft undertakings. The three major socialist reforms – that is, the socialist revolution of the ownership of means of production was basically accomplished in 1956, and following this, the socialist revolutions on the political front and the ideological front were carried out last year. . . . It is now necessary to launch a technical revolution so that we may overtake Britain in fifteen years or a little longer.

The technical component of the forty-point Programme was also reformulated by Chairman Mao Tse-tung in the autumn of 1958, and put forward in the form of an 'Eight Point Charter' of Scientific Farming in China. These eight points which are still widely emphasised were as follows:

Soil: Deep ploughing and soil improvement, overall survey, planning and rational utilisation of land.
Fertilizer: Rational application of fertilizer, with the kind and quantity according to the type of crop, nature and condition of the soil and needs at the different stages of crop growth.
Water conservation: Construction of projects for irrigation and drainage, and rational utilisation of water.
Seed selection: The use of seed from high-quality strains.
Close planting: The maxium number of plants that can be grown per unit area through close-planting and intercropping

while still obtaining adequate nutrition, sunlight and air.

Plant protection: Prevention and treatment of plant diseases and elimination of weeds, insect pests and harmful birds and animals.

Reform of tools: Reform of farm tools and the use of machinery to raise labour productivity.

Field management: Timely cultivation, irrigation and application of fertilizer and meticulous care of the crops throughout the growing period.

Detailed instructions were formulated on each of these points and widely distributed with emphasis on modification and adaptation to local conditions. Probably the agricultural extension services in many developing countries have tried to spread similar information, but there is a lot of difference between persuading a small illiterate farmer through technical arguments and a political campaign in which technical advice reaches the farmer through his own local leaders and institutional framework, with the full force of an ideological command.

EXTENT OF MODERNISATION

According to some estimates, by 1972 roughly 20 per cent of China's cultivated lands (i.e. 25 million hectares) had modernised agriculture.[5] These areas, located in about a dozen different regions and called 'areas of high and stable yields', have mechanical irrigation, improved seed varieties, more chemical fertilizer and selective mechanisation. In this modernised segment of Chinese agriculture, agricultural yields have increased three to four times, exceeding the targets laid down in the National Development Programme of 1956. Neither floods nor drought can now influence production in these areas to any great extent and possibilities of double and triple cropping have greatly increased. There are some other pockets of modernisation, particularly around urban centres in different parts of the country and in areas where cultivation is not possible without modern machinery. Efforts are now being made to extend this process of technical change through 'four basic changes; irrigation, electrification, chemicalisation and mechanisation' to other regions which are in varying phases of transition.

The pace of technological change after 1972 has been rapid and by 1975, the areas with 'high and stable yields' probably accounted for 25 per cent of China's cultivated land. This is reflected in the sharp increase in grain production since 1973. Total grain output in China, which increased from 200 million tons in the mid-1960s to 240 million tons in 1970, began to stagnate, partly due to bad weather, between 240 and 250 million tons in the next three years. Since 1973, however, grain production has increased sharply to 275 million tons in 1974 and to an estimated 285 million tons in 1975.

The areas in which the technical transformation of agriculture has already been achieved were not deliberately chosen by the State. The political and social re-organisation of the rural population, referred to in Chapter 2, prepared the ground for rapid progress in all parts of the country. But in areas where growing conditions were more favourable and yields relatively high, the communes were able to generate a surplus to procure irrigation equipment and fertilizer and to expand facilities for education and training and for sideline activities. The State Government at the Provincial and County levels was ready to offer a package of technical services, available inputs and farm machinery on the basis of requirements indicated by the communes. Even in areas where growing conditions are less favourable, efforts have been made to increase productivity through irrigation and mechanisation. The well-known campaign of 'Learning from Tachai' is primarily intended to demonstrate that even in areas with unfavourable natural conditions the highest possible yields can be obtained with hard work and a scientific approach to farming.

A more rapid pace of technical change in certain areas does create the problem of income disparities between different regions, at least in the initial phases. This is partly resolved in China through the system of grain pricing. The price paid to the communes for grain supplied within the assigned quota is relatively low – 9.8 Yuan for 100 catties of rice in Kwantung Province for example, compared to 13.9 Yuan for 100 catties of 'high price grain', i.e. for quantities supplied above the quota. This differential, while providing incentives to surplus communes to supply additional grain over and above the quota, also helps the deficit communes which receive grain from the State at relatively lower prices (10 Yuan for 100 catties). Since most of the less prosperous communes are located in remote areas, involving additional transport costs for carrying grain, the implicit subsidy is somewhat larger.

The success achieved by China in initiating the technical transformation of its agricultural sector within a relatively short period of fifteen years is reflected not only in the overall results achieved in terms of grain production or improvement of rural life discussed in Chapter 5, but also in many specific indicators of technical change. These include:

- the increase in area under irrigation and the resultant increase in cropping intensity;
- the expansion of area under improved seed and other related improvements in farming techniques;
- the supply and production of a larger quantity of chemical fertilizers; and
- the gradual mechanisation of agricultural operations and the progress made in the domestic manufacture of tractors and other forms of agricultural machinery.

Each of these elements of modernisation and technical change is, of course, closely related to the other, and better results can be obtained only if they are carefully integrated in a package. Improved seed can hardly produce larger crops without an adequate and timely supply of fertilizer and water. Similarly, double and triple cropping generally requires improved varieties with shorter growing periods, but the harvesting and replanting operations can seldom be managed without agricultural machinery. The remaining part of this chapter contains a brief review of these four elements of technical transformation of China's agriculture but it is important to highlight two important lessons of China's technological progress.

First, within a given locality the rate of technical change is fairly uniform and widespread. Since the land is collectively owned and cultivated, the spread of technology is not related to size of holding as in many other developing countries in which the large and medium-scale farmers have succeeded in modernising their farms but the small farmer has been left out. In China, the entire area within a commune is cultivated on the basis of the best knowledge that is available. Similarly, available machinery and fertilizer are shared by all the members. There are elaborate and efficient arrangements to share knowledge of new techniques or seeds or problems between production teams and production brigades within a commune, and between different communes in a region. The gap between research and its application and between the best yield obtained on demonstration plots and at the farm level is therefore being constantly narrowed.

Second, the fruits of technical progress are distributed equally within a commune. There are differences in income levels between production brigades and production teams, but these are relatively minor when compared to the serious imbalance in rural incomes in other developing countries in which new technology has reached only the large or medium-sized farms.

WATER CONTROL AND MANAGEMENT

Of all the factors that account for the success of agricultural and social development in China, the most important has been the ability to control, manage and use the water resources effectively. Historically, about one-fourth to one-third of China's cultivated land was subject to periodical flooding and China's rainfall is not evenly distributed between regions or from year to year. The National Agricultural Development Programme, formulated in 1956, placed primary emphasis on flood control and irrigation and called for the elimination of ordinary flood and drought within twelve years by the building of medium-sized and large water-conservancy projects and the harnessing of medium-sized and large rivers by the State. It also set a goal of expanding the irrigated areas from 390 million mou in 1955 to 900 million mou by 1968, and of expanding the capacity of irrigation facilities to deal with drought to between 30 and 50 days in most areas, but between 50 and 70 days in places suitable for double-crop paddy fields. The programme also emphasised the need for power generation through small and medium-sized hydro-electric stations and their co-ordination with medium and large power stations built by the State, to increase the supply of electricity to the countryside.

In the 1950s, water conservation efforts in China included some very large projects undertaken by the State to control and regulate the main rivers (the San Menshia Dam project on the Yellow River, the Ching River flood detention project, the Szechuan dam on the Yangtze River and several dams and reservoirs on the upstream tributaries of the Huai River) and thousands of small and medium-sized projects undertaken by the co-operatives to improve draining, construct reservoirs and embankments and dig wells and ponds. In the 1960s, while labour-intensive efforts to control floods and expand irrigation facilities continued, there was a substantial increase in the number of pumps and other irrigation equipment and a corresponding increase in the consumption of electricity in the rural areas and in the total area using mechanical irrigation.

The latest available data on total cultivated area, irrigated area, rural electrification and the area covered by irrigation and draining equipment is present in Table 3.2 on page 32.

The total area under irrigation is estimated to have increased more than threefold, in the 26-year period from 1949 to 1975 – from 240 million mou to 735 million mou against the target of 900 set in the forty-point National Programme. This increase is much larger than the increase in total cultivated area, which is estimated to have increased by one-third, from 1468.2 million mou (97.8 million hectares) in 1949 to 1950 million mou (130 million hectares) in 1975. In 1949, according to official Chinese sources, only 4.2 million mou (0.28 million hectares) had access to mechanical irrigation and draining equipment. This increased slowly to 8.3 million mou in 1955, but then rose more sharply to 35 million mou in 1965 and to 109.5 million mou (7.3 million hectares) in 1975. The figure for 1975 is 15 per cent of total irrigated area or about 735 million mou. The installed power capacity of electricity and diesel for irrigation and draining equipment increased from 97,000 h.p. in 1949 to 560,000 h.p. in 1957, 2.3 million in 1961, 20 million in 1971 and 30 million in 1975. Similarly, the number of water pumps (10 h.p. on average) increased slowly to 100,000 by 1965, but jumped to 600,000 in 1971 and 1.5 million in 1975. The strategy reflected in these numbers makes a great deal of economic sense. It is much more expensive and difficult to bring new land under cultivation than to improve the cropping intensity of the land already under cultivation.

Similarly, in the expansion of irrigation facilities it is much more practical to rely initially on gravity irrigation through canals and aqueducts and on small reservoirs and dams and then gradually to provide new sources of energy and equipment, financed partly by the surplus generated by these projects in order to make better use of the water that has been stored or diverted.

According to some Chinese estimates,[6] the cost of irrigating a mou of land by small ponds, small dams and water pumps is 7 to 10 Yuan but it is 52 Yuan by larger reservoirs. But these figures must be treated as indicative since actual costs will depend on the terrain, the possibility for gravity flows and the need for pumping.

One of the most impressive irrigation projects in China is the Red Flag Canal in Linhsien County in Honan Province. This was a relatively poor region with recurring drought and occasional floods. The total population of the county is 700,000 and the area 2000 sq km, but its cultivable land is only 60,000 hectares of which less than 1000 hectares had some seasonal irrigation before the liberation. In dry periods, people living in the higher reaches of the county had to walk down several miles to get drinking water. After liberation, they constructed in 1957–8, three medium-sized reservoirs and three canals, 13.5 km long, to store up some water in the upper valleys, but in years of low rainfall the reservoirs could not be filled. They decided, after further investigation and a great deal of discussion, that the only long-term solution of their problems was to divert water through a canal from the Changho River flowing just beyond the northern mountain ranges. The construction of this canal was started in February 1960, with the equivalent of 10,000 workers toiling full-time for nine years. In practice, the intensity of work varied with the season and up to 30,000 workers were employed on the project during peak working periods. The project involved 134 tunnels with a total length of 24 km, 150 aquaducts with a total length of 6.5 km and the removal of 16 million cubic metres of earth and stone. The total length of the main canal and its three subsidiaries is 1500 km. The project included 700 pumping stations to irrigate higher lands and sixty-five medium and small electric stations with a capacity of 10,000 kW. Irrigation is now available for 40,000 hectares or two-thirds of the total cultivable area and the yield of wheat has gone up from less than 1 ton per

Table 3.2 Information on total cultivated and irrigated areas, areas using mechanical irrigation and draining equipment and extent of rural electrification

Year	Total cultivated area (million ha)	Total irrigated area (million ha)	Total area using I & D equipment (million ha)	Installed capacity h.p. equiv (million h.p.)	Number of tube pump wells (million)	Rural electricity consumption (million Kwh.)
1949	97.8	16.0	0.28	0.1		
1952	107.9	21.3	0.33			43
1957	111.8	29.6	—	0.56		108
1965	102.2	34.6	2.33	7.5	0.1	2592
1971	127.0	42.6	6.60	20	0.6	
1975	130.6	49.0	7.30	30 +	1.5	

Sources:

Cultivated area 1949–57 State Statistical Bureau, Ten Great Years (Peking: Foreign Languages Press, 1960).
1965 Chinese Agricultural Bulletin 1966, No. 9, p. 16, quoted in Chao, Agricultural Production in Communist China, 1949–1965, p. 306.
1971 Henle, Report on China's Agriculture (FAO, 1974).
1975 Author's own estimate.

Irrigated area 1949–57 Ten Great Years, op. cit., p. 130. Total given for 1957 is 520 but it is admitted that for 150 million mou drought resistance was inadequate – only half of 150 million mou is assumed here to be effective. Summary Report by Ho Chi-feng at 1957 National Farmland Irrigation Conference (date not revealed), *China Water Conservancy*, No. 9, 14 September 1957 cited in Carin, *Irrigation Scheme in Communist China* (U.R.I., 1963) p. A-7.

1965   See Kuo, *The Technical Transformation of Agriculture in Communist China*, p. 80 for official Chinese sources.

1971   *Reassessment of the Chinese Economy*, U.S. Congress, Joint Economic Committee, 1975, p. 360 for official Chinese sources. (This is the official figure for 1972.)

1975   *Peking Review*, No. 50, 12 December 1957, p. 17 states total irrigated area showed an average yearly increase of 24 million mou between 1972 and 1975, i.e. 96 million mou + 639 = 735 million mou.

Area using
I & D power
equipment

1949–52   See Chao, op. cit. p. 124, for official Chinese sources.
1965   NCNA 16 July 1965 communique on the National Conference on Drainage and Irrigation Machinery in United States Agricultural Attache Office, Agricultural Information on Mainland China 1953–1967 (USAAO) Reel 5 p. 94.

1971   NCNA – English 7 January 1974 in SPRCP 1974–03, p. 118.
1975   *Peking Review*, No. 1, pp. 10–11, 3 January 1976. Selections from the PRC Press (SPRCP) American Consulate H.K.

Installed I & D
capacity

1949   NCNA 21 December 1961 in Carin, *Irrigation Scheme in Communist China* (URI) p. A–9.
1957   *Reassessment*, op. cit. p. 360 using official Chinese sources.
1965   *Peking Review*, No. 1, pp. 10–11, 3 January 1976.
1971   See 1957 source.
1975   See 1965 source.

Number of tube
pump wells

1965   *Peking Review*, No. 1, pp. 10–11, 3 January 1976.
1971   *Reassessment*, op. cit, using official Chines sources.
1975   NCNA in *Financial Times*, 3 December 1975.

Rural electricity
consumption

1949–57   Chao, op. cit. p. 139.
1965   *Radio Peking*, 2 December 1965 in USAAO Reel 5, p. 92.

hectare to 3.75 tons per hectare. In 1975 the county produced a surplus of 23,000 tons of grain over and above the needs of its population of 700,000. In addition, the supply of cheap electricity has facilitated the setting up of many industrial units by the county and by the fifteen communes located in the county and their production brigades. Education and health facilities have also expanded. There are sixteen senior high schools, 230 junior high schools and 690 primary schools. Every commune has a hospital and every brigade has a clinic.

The most striking aspect of this project is perhaps the fact that it was largely designed, executed and financed from local resources, with very little machinery or modern equipment. The State provided some supplies such as dynamite to blow up rocks and later on equipment for pumps and electric stations, but the entire labour force was provided by the communes. Each production team or brigade was expected to supply workers in proportion to the anticipated benefits from the project. The salary of these workers was met from the income of the teams or brigades while they worked on the project.

In every part of China there are countless examples of similar projects, constructed by the local population through their own resources and a mass mobilisation of labour using simple tools and local techniques.

In overall terms, the total area under irrigation is now about 40 per cent of the cultivated area, and of the irrigated area at least 15 per cent has mechanical equipment. In the next ten to fifteen years, there is scope for a further 50 per cent increase in irrigated area, bringing the total to at least 60 per cent of the cultivated area.

AGRICULTURAL TECHNOLOGY AND IMPROVED SEEDS

Even before the liberation in 1949 China had, under the Ministry of Agriculture, National Bureaux of Research for Agriculture, Animal Husbandry, Fisheries and Forestry, and a wide range of institutions and research stations at provincial and lower levels. But as is typical in many other developing countries, these bureaux and institutions were poorly equipped and inadequately financed. They did not produce any systematic results and whatever they did produce seldom reached the farm level.

In the early 1950s, several agencies under the Ministry of Agriculture began more intensive work in different agricultural fields and a number of agricultural colleges were set up. The Chinese Academy of Agricultural Science was established in March 1957 to co-ordinate the work of various agricultural colleges and research organisations. The Academy has created about two dozen specialised research institutes for different crops with branches and experiment stations at regional, provincial and lower levels. Most communes have their own small peasant research groups. The main function of these research stations is to disseminate information received from higher levels in the form of pamphlets and posters and to train farmers. Some communes have started regular programmes of training which bring together fifteen, twenty or thirty workers for a period ranging from a week to a month. Some of these training courses cover basic agricultural techniques while others may be designed to deal with special problems and needs of the locality. In practice, almost every production brigade has at least a few trained workers. Those who do well in these training programmes may be selected to become research workers at the research stations.

In the introduction of modern technology, China has relied on the principle of 'walking on two legs'. This principle has many applications in different aspects of Chinese life but in this context it means relying on the old and the traditional method while developing new and more scientific methods. It also emphasises continuous interaction between the farmer and the scientist, the farmer learning better techniques from the scientist and the scientist going to the villages to see the problems at first hand.

The total cultivated area of China has increased by only 33 per cent since 1949 – from 98 million hectares in 1949 to 130 million hectares in 1975 but the area sown has gone up from 141 million hectares in 1952 to 200 million hectares in 1975.[7] In other words, at least 50 per cent of the cultivated area is multiple-cropped, including about 10 per cent which produces three crops.

Like many other parts of Asia, China has accorded high priority, particularly in the 1960s, to the introduction of improved seed in order to achieve higher yields. There are literally hundreds of varieties of each crop being continuously tested, developed and exchanged and there is no satisfactory way of making an estimate of the area covered by improved varieties at a given point of time. The definition of what is an improved seed also changes. As new varieties are evolved, varieties considered improved by previous standards can be treated either way. According to official sources, improved strains are now used in over 80 per cent of China's rice-growing areas and over 70 per cent of the wheat-growing areas in the Yellow River Valley.[8]

By the mid-1970s, the highest yield obtained from improved varieties under experimental conditions was 6 – 7 tons per hectare for rice and 3 – 4 tons per hectare for wheat. Table 3.3, however, provides an overall view of the average increase in yields obtained in four major crops between 1957 and 1975. The increase, of course, is not entirely due to improved seed, but that is certainly an important factor.

Table 3.3

	Area sown to grains (million hectares)			Production (million metric tons)				Yield (tons/hectare)			
	1952	1957[1]	1971[2]1975[3]	1952[1]	1957[1]	1971[2]1975[3]		1952	1957[1]	1971	1975
Wheat	24.8	27.5	30+		24	38			0.86	1.26		
Rice	28.4	32.2	40+		87	120			2.69	3.00		
Misc.												
Gr.	50.5	50.6	60+		53	69			1.04	1.15		
Tubers	8.7	10.5	15+		22	24			2.09	2.50		
	112.4	120.8	145	160	154[1]	186[1]	251[4] 285	1.37	1.54	1.72	1.78

1. *Ten Great Years*, official figures op. cit.
2. Unofficial estimates given to Henle (op. cit.) by Bank of China.
3. Author's estimates based on semi-official briefing.
4. Official Chinese figure, *Peking Review*, No. 1 (5 January 1973) p. 13.

In practice, due to a wide variety of growing conditions and problems, some areas have adopted varieties which give lower yields but are more suitable to local climatic conditions. For example, high-yielding maize varieties grown in northern China are too tall for the more windy climate of the area around the Yangtze River. Similarly, areas subject to flooding need a taller stem to keep the crop above water. In areas where double and triple cropping is possible, the Chinese have developed rice varieties with shorter growing periods. These are kept in the nurseries for a longer period and thus permit transplanting soon after the early rice is harvested in early August.[9] This involves a tremendous effort and organisational ability to complete the harvest of one crop and the transplanting of the other within a fortnight. Almost the entire population of a commune has to be mobilised for such an effort.

The average yield of the major crops given in Table 3.3 is less than half of the best yields obtained under experimental conditions. The general level of agricultural technology in China, although higher than in most other developing countries, is still in its middle stages, compared to Japan or some Western countries. There is thus room for further improvement in agricultural technology and for increasing average yields. Such improvements will depend mainly on a larger supply of fertiliser and on the pace of mechanisation. As the next two sections clearly bring out, the main thrust of China's agricultural efforts in the next few years seems to be in these two sub-sectors.

FERTILIZERS

China's experience with natural fertilizers is many centuries old. In the Yuan dynasty (thirteenth and fourteenth centuries), the Chinese were using grasses, roots, night soil and mud from ponds and sewers to fertilize their fields. By the fifteenth and sixteenth centuries, they began to use various commercial fertilizers like bean-cakes, dried fish, limestone and pig manures. Over the next four centuries, the availability of natural fertilizer increased with the rise in human and animal population. According to official figures, in 1952 about 60 per cent of cultivated land received an average of 750 kg of natural fertilizer per mou (11.25 tons per hectare). This would be equal to 729 million tons in gross weight and 2.76 million tons in terms of plant nutrients. The use of natural fertilizer is estimated to have increased by at least 54 per cent to 4.25 million nutrient tons between 1952 and 1966 and by a further 42 per cent to 6.07 million tons between 1966 and 1972, or a total increase of 120 per cent in the twenty-year period. This level apparently provided about 4 kg of plant nutrients per mou of cultivated area (compared to 2.80 kg in 1966 and 1.66 kg in 1952).[10]

The increase in the use of natural fertilizer in China in the past twenty years is very impressive and could be regarded as a major factor in increasing yields during the period. But the collection and transport of natural fertilizer requires a great deal of labour, often in busy periods; besides, there are natural limits to the supply of natural fertilizers. From the early 1960s, China began to accord high priority to the domestic production of chemical fertilizer through small and medium-size plants to meet local needs and some large plants using modern technology. The total production of chemical fertilizer has increased from a nominal quantity of 27,000 tons in 1949 to 1.77 million tons (total nitrogen and phosphate) in 1959 and 25 million tons in 1975, or about 4.62 nutrient tons.

From 1952 onwards, China also began to import fertilizer to supplement domestic production. Fertilizer imports have risen steadily from 128,000 tons in 1952 to 1 million tons in 1957 and about 4 million tons in 1971–2. Imports of fertilizer were curtailed after 1973 because of a sharp increase in prices.

The total availability of fertilizer in China is indicated in Table 3.4.

Since about 60 per cent of China's domestic production of fertilizer is in small plants producing a large variety of different fertilizers with crop nutrients ranging from 10 to 21 per cent, it is difficult to make an accurate estimate of the total crop nutrients provided by chemical fertilizers. But the average percentage of crop nutrient from domestic production would be about 18–19 per cent and that from imports about 30 per cent. On this basis the total estimated supply of 27 million tons of chemical fertilizer in 1975 would be equal to 5.22 million nutrient tons. In other words, by 1975, China was already obtaining about 45 per cent of crop nutrients from chemical fertilizers compared to only 2 per cent in 1952. Even then, the total supply of fertilizer – both chemical and natural – works out in 1975 to about 86 kg per cultivated hectare or 56 kg per sown hectare. This is less than one-quarter of that used in Japan or half that regarded as optimum for tropical crops like rice.[11] These figures indicate China's potential for agricultural productivity.

In 1973–4, partly as a result of the sharp increase in fertilizer prices and partly in recognition of the growing importance of chemical fertilizers in its agriculture, China concluded contracts

Table 3.4 Supply of chemical fertilizers (1949–75) – (1000 tons)

| | Domestic production | | | | |
	Nitrogen	Phosphate	Total	Imports	Total Supply
1949	27	–	27	–	27
1952	188	–	188	128	316
1957	751	120	871	996	1,867
1965	6,900	2,000	8,900	1,989	10,889
1972	12,000	7,900	19,900	4,000	23,900
1975	15,000	10,000	25,000	2,000	27,000

Sources
Domestic production
1949, 1952, 1957   *Ten Great Years.*
1965   Chao, op. cit. p. 317.
1972   Stavis, op. cit. p. 41.
1975   Author's estimates based on semi-official briefing.

Imports
1949–65   Liu, *China's Fertilizer Economy* (Edinburgh Press, 1971) p. 50.
1972   Stavis, op. cit. p. 41.
1975   Author's estimates based on semi-official briefing.

for setting up thirteen large fertilizer factories to produce urea and other concentrated fertilizers. These plants, when in operation, will increase the domestic production of chemical fertilizer by two-thirds and could become one of the most important factors in raising agricultural production. The setting up of these large fertilizer plants was also encouraged in part by the recent upsurge of the petroleum industry in China.

It is significant that in emphasising the larger use of chemical fertilizer, China has not de-emphasised the use of natural fertilizer. Despite an unprecedented increase of 40 per cent a year in the supply of chemical fertilizer between 1949 and 1975, the use of natural fertilizer in terms of plant nutrients has, as already mentioned, also increased by 120 per cent (or 3.5 per cent a year) since 1952. The Chinese experience clearly shows that chemical fertilizer used in conjunction with organic manure can lead to a much higher response than that from the same quantity of plant nutrients obtained from chemical fertilizer only.[12]

MECHANISATION

Another important indicator of agricultural modernisation in China is the rapid pace of mechanisation, particularly since the mid-1960s. As in all other aspects of agriculture, the Chinese first concentrated, in the early 1950s, on increasing the supply and improving the quality of traditional tools and implements. In the late 1950s, they began to manufacture simple irrigation equipment. The use of tractors in the 1950s was relatively limited and was confined to State farms and services provided by the agricultural machinery stations. By 1961, the total number of tractors in use was about 90,000 and gradually increased to 130,000 by 1965. From 1964, after a great deal of experimentation with various models and sizes, the domestic manufacture of tractors was started, and increased very rapidly. In 1972, the total number of tractors for farm use was 2.6 times that in 1965, and the number manufactured in 1974 was reported to be 5.4 times that in 1964 (i.e. 118,000). The total number of tractors in use by 1975 is estimated at about 500,000.

Normally, a standard tractor unit of 15 h.p. can service about 100 hectares of land, leaving about one-third to one-half of the total time for use as transport which is very extensive in China. On this basis, the estimated availability of 500,000 tractors should be adequate for 50 million hectares of land or about 25 per cent of the total sown area of 200 million hectares. But since a much larger proportion of tractors manufactured after 1965 is the small garden variety, the total area cultivated would be lower, probably about 40 million hectares or 20 per cent of the sown area. In other words, at least *one-fifth of China's agriculture has already been mechanised.*

Agricultural mechanisation in China is not confined to tractors. Considerable progress has been made in the manufacture of various other machines and equipment for threshing, crushing, harvesting, plant protection and, more recently, rice transplanting. Data on these machines are not available but this equipment is heavily concentrated in the 'high and stable yield

Table 3.5 Production and use of tractors in China

	Annual domestic production (A)	Total in use (B)
1949	–	401
1952	–	2,006
1957	–	24,629
1958	957	45,330
1961	15,200	90,000
1964	21,900	123,000
1965	N.A.	130,000
1971	N.A.	220,000
1972	N.A.	338,000
1974	118,000	404,000
1975	N.A.	500,000

Sources: Column A: 1958, 1961, 1964 See Chao, Table 4.3, p. 107 for
official Chinese sources.
1974 *Peking Review*, No. 41, (10 October 1975) p.
10.
Column B: 1949–65. See Chao, Table 4.3, p. 107 for official
Chinese sources.
1971 *Peking Review*, No. 46 (1972) pp. 16–17.
1972. Cheng Shih, *A Glance at China's Economy*, p.
18.
1974 Estimate by author.
1975 Estimate by author.

areas' already mentioned, and in areas close to urban or
industrial centres.

China's success in the selective mechanisation of agriculture
should not, however, be judged simply in terms of the increase in
the number of tractors and other machines but in three other
significant aspects of its mechanisation policy.

First, the Chinese began to mechanise agriculture *after*
achieving a significant diversification of the rural economy in
which a sizeable proportion of the rural population had already
been absorbed in non-agricultural activities and many communes were facing labour shortages in peak seasons. There is also
continuing emphasis on small hand-operated tractors. Increasing mechanisation has not therefore adversely affected the
employment situation.

Secondly, the mechanisation of agriculture has been financed by the communes and brigades largely from their own savings, and the total 'demand' for tractors and other machinery is reported to be higher than the State can meet. This is partly because the prices of agricultural machinery are relatively low, not only in comparison with international standards but even by Chinese standards. The distribution of agricultural machinery is controlled by various quota systems operated at different levels. Because of the relative shortage of machinery the utilisation rate of tractors has improved considerably.[13]

Thirdly the whole range of agricultural machinery is manufactured within China. Hand-tractors are manufactured in small urban centres and now increasingly in the county workshops. There is virtually no import of agricultural machinery.

From 1975 the emphasis has been shifting from selective mechanisation to full-scale mechanisation. Chairman Mao's famous slogan, 'The fundamental way out for agriculture lies in mechanisation', is now being implemented on a bigger scale. A National Conference on 'Learning from Tachai in Agriculture' was held in Peking in October 1975 and accepted the 'basic mechanisation of agriculture by 1980' as one of the most important goals.

'Basic mechanisation' in this context means mechanising roughly 70 per cent of power in agricultural operations including ploughing, cultivation, harvesting and food processing. Hua Kuo-feng, who took over as Prime Minister of China in April 1976 and as Chairman of the Party in October 1976, in his summing-up Report to the Conference, called for 70 per cent mechanisation in all major operations in agriculture, forestry, animal husbandry, sideline occupations and fisheries. Some extracts from this comprehensive Report are reproduced below:

Farmland capital construction has been carried out on a large scale, and during the past four years some 100 million people have taken part in each winter – spring period, bringing an average of 1.6 million more hectares of land each year under irrigation. The rate of mechanisation of agriculture has been gradually stepped up. The amount of irrigation and drainage equipment, chemical fertilizer and tractors supplied in the past four years exceeded the total supplied in the previous fifteen years, and a number of production brigades, communes and counties have attained a relatively high degree of mechanisation. Mass scientific experiment in farming has spread far and wide. Three provinces and two municipalities, forty-four prefectures and 725 counties have topped their targets for per-hectare yield of grain set in the National Programme for Agricultural Development. Another eleven provinces and one municipality are nearing their respective targets. Thirty counties in the north have reached the target set for areas south of the Yangtze River, six of them topping the 7.5 ton-per-hectare mark, and four counties in the south have doubled the yield set by the programme.

In order to build themselves into Tachai-type counties, all counties must map out over-all plans for their farmland capital construction. These should centre on improving the soil and building water conservancy projects, while the mountains, rivers, farmland, forests and roads should be tackled in a comprehensive way. We must see clearly the main direction of our attack and concentrate strength to fight a 'war of annihilation'. The projects should be carried out in stages, and check-ups and summing-up of experience should be made regularly. Attention must be paid to suiting local conditions and getting practical results, not seeking achievements in form. With large-scale farmland capital construction under way, there will be more and more inter-brigade and inter-commune projects. The brigades and communes must strengthen unified organisation and leadership of these projects, practise mutual help and mutual benefit and co-ordinate their work well. Conditions must be created for the gradual spread of the county, commune and brigade farmland capital construction contingents, a new emerging thing specialised in transforming nature and vigorously building socialism.

The equipping of agriculture with machinery is the decisive condition for a big and integrated expansion of farming, forestry and animal husbandry. In the course of building Tachai-type counties throughout the country, the provinces, municipalities and autonomous regions must energetically develop their own farm machinery industry in the light of local conditions so as to supply the communes and production brigades with equipment and other products needed for the mechanisation of agriculture. The prefectures and counties, for their part, must according to their own resources and other conditions set up small industrial enterprises producing iron and steel, coal, chemical fertilizer, cement and machinery in order to provide the rural areas with more farm machinery, chemical fertilizer and insecticide suited to local needs. We must publicise among the masses Chairman Mao's teaching that *the fundamental way out for agriculture lies in mechanisation*, bring the enthusiasm and initiative of the hundreds of millions of people into full play, work energetically for the technical transformation of agriculture and gradually raise the level of mechanised farming in a planned way. We must train a mighty contingent of people for mechanised farming, people who are both workers and peasants and well acquainted with modern techniques. The development of farm mechanisation will greatly raise labour productivity in agriculture and give the peasants plenty of time to develop a diversified economy and build a new, prosperous and rich socialist countryside. It will also have a great significance in bringing into play the role of the people's commune as an organisation that combines industry, agriculture, commerce, education and military affairs, in enabling the commune to display its superiority – big in size and with a high degree of public ownership – and in narrowing the differences between town and country, between worker and peasant and between manual and mental labour. Therefore, the various departments concerned under the State Council and the leading organs of the provinces, prefectures and counties must make very great efforts to speed up the progress of this work, make various practical arrangements, take effective measures, check on its progress every year and sum up experience, so as to ensure that the great task of mechanising agriculture will be accomplished in the main by 1980.[14]

In many ways, this Conference marks a milestone in China's strategy for rural development and will not only influence the pace of mechanisation but the whole pattern of future development of the country through its impact on the nature and rate of industrial production, the rates of savings and investments of the rural population and the mechanisation of transport. According to indications so far available, the overall pace of mechanisation will be controlled by the State through co-ordination at the county level where State-operated plants for the manufacture of relatively complex machinery and parts will be located. The communes and brigades will produce and assemble less sophisticated equipment and also provide the resources to finance the programme by increasing savings out of larger production. Each commune and its units will decide the precise nature and pace of mechanisation according to its own requirements, geographic and climatic conditions and financial resources.

The National Conference[15] on 'Learning from Tachai' was followed by many Provincial Conferences to set provincial goals and policies for mechanisation and agricultural yields in the light of local conditions and needs. In addition, a million cadres have been sent to all parts of the country to communicate these decisions and strengthen the mass movement of 'Learning from Tachai', and to help the campaign to rectify and improve local leadership.

4

The People's Communes

The Chinese commune has played a very important role in the economic, social and political life of rural China since 1958. Almost every visitor to China has the opportunity to visit one or more communes and a great deal has been written in the past few years about communes, their history, structure, operations, achievements and problems. This chapter does not attempt to present a comprehensive view of the people's communes but a brief account for those who are not already familiar with literature on China. It also concentrates on certain key functions and aspects of the commune which are critical for determining the relevance of the Chinese experience for other developing countries.

There are, of course, considerable variations in the internal arrangements that have evolved in various communes as also in the income levels and social services provided by different communes. These variations do not, however, affect the validity of the typical pattern or the overall conclusions about the results so far achieved. Comprehensive data, covering all the 50,000 communes, are not so far available, but there is considerable information available on individual communes in many parts of the country, which provides a fairly dependable view of economic and social indicators of rural life in China. Information on some forty-one communes located in many different parts of the country, some relatively prosperous and some not so prosperous, is summarised in Appendix B.

A Chinese commune is not a large agricultural co-operative but a composite unit of local government that encompasses the whole range of economic, social, administrative and political functions for the rural community. Its essential purpose is to organise and mobilise the rural population, to develop their land and other resources in order to meet their essential needs on the principle of self-reliance while at the same time reducing social inequalities and creating a rural society based on justice and equality.

Land reforms, even when they are drastic and succeed in achieving a minimum of equality in the distribution of land and other resources among the rural population, create only certain essential pre-conditions for rural development. These must be followed by appropriate institutional and organisational arrangements that will help to organise the rural population for each successive stage of rural development. In China these arrangements, as already explained in Chapter 1, were evolved over a period of six years, through four different stages, and culminated in the system of people's communes in 1958. Several important modifications and changes were introduced in the system in 1961-2, but in the past fifteen years the communes have proved their institutional viability.

The most significant and, in practice, the most difficult step, from private ownership to collective ownership[1] of land, was taken in China with the creation of advanced producers' co-operatives. In these 740,000 advanced co-operatives, most of which were created in 1956, the income received by members was no longer related to land ownership but to the amount of work done, but these units were too small in size to carry out larger irrigation projects or to diversify the rural economy by undertaking industrial and other non-agricultural activities. At the same time, the extension of economic activities in rural areas could not go on without being integrated with appropriate administrative and political units. The people's communes were created in 1958 by merging the advanced co-operatives with the lowest administrative units traditionally called Hsiangs (townships). Initially, about six or seven advanced co-operatives and three Hsiangs were merged into one commune to form a total of 26,000 communes. But in 1962, the 26,000 communes were again sub-divided into 74,000 communes, each largely corresponding to one Hsiang, or old market town and its natural marketing area. The communes, even after being sub-divided, have remained large organisational units. As already mentioned, some communes have again been amalgamated and in 1975 the total number of communes was reported to be 50,000.[2] These communes are linked to the Central Government through 2000 counties and twenty-two provinces. The system apparently has now been extended to various autonomous regions of Central Asia which depend essentially on livestock. The area covered by State farms in different parts of the country is very small – probably about 2 per cent of the total cultivable land.

THE ORGANISATION AND FUNCTIONS OF COMMUNES

The size of a commune varies enormously depending on the density of population in a particular area in proportion to available land. I have personally visited communes with populations of 80,000 and a land area of 8000 hectares, and some visitors have reported on a commune in a remote area with only 600 people. But these are exceptions. The majority of communes, as can be seen from data given in Appendix B, have a population ranging from 10,000 to 40,000 (i.e. 2500 to 10,000 households)[3] and a land-holding ranging from 800 to 4000 hectares. The proportion of land-holding to the population of the commune is of course not uniform and some communes, as shown in Appendix B, Items 13 and 38, has only 4067 hectares of land for a population of 70,000 while another commune has 6000 hectares for a population of 18,000. But the average pattern of land-holding provides about 0.2 hectare of cultivable land per person and only 0.1 hectare in densely populated areas.

A commune is divided into a number of production brigades, which are further sub-divided into production teams. As with the size of a commune, there are wide differences in the number of brigades and teams in a commune. In some densely-populated areas, a commune may have thirty to thirty-five brigades and 300 to 400 production teams, but some have only five to ten brigades and only fifty to 100 production teams.

A *production team* often consists of a natural village or cluster of houses with twenty, thirty or forty families or 100 to 200 members, cultivating anything from 10 to 40 hectares, depending on population density in relation to available land. The production team is the basic production and accounting unit which owns the land and is responsible for all the decisions involving the deployment of available manpower, managing production and distributing the income generated by the production team. The overall planning of production is subject to certain guidelines such as quotas for grain and basic commodities which must be sold to the State at fixed prices and minimum or maximum quotas for certain other agricultural products such as fruit, vegetables, fish or meat, but the production team has some flexibility or discretion in meeting different quotas or exceeding certain quotas. Similarly, the production team has substantial autonomy in making investment decisions involving its own labour and savings, such as buying agricultural machinery, planting an orchard or improving its irrigation facilities. In practice, the production team is still the most important unit of rural organisation in China's countryside.

The *production brigade* co-ordinates the annual production plans of the teams on the basis of quotas assigned by the commune and allocates certain agricultural inputs such as fertilizer and pumps. But its more important functions are to undertake investment and development activities on a scale that is too large for the production team. The brigades may set up livestock farms, vegetable gardens, fruit orchards and small-scale industries. In addition, it provides certain social services like primary schools and health clinics. Brigades may also organise credit co-operatives or militia units; in some cases, they may serve as the accounting unit, but these are not common. The brigade also serves as the seat of the party branch and is thus the lowest level at which the party operates through direct contact with the rural population.

The *commune* not only co-ordinates, supervises and guides all these activities of production teams and production brigades but discharges supplementary functions which are beyond their capacity or scope. It undertakes larger projects requiring a considerable workforce or substantial financial resources, such as large water-conservancy projects or rural roads and industrial units. In addition, it provides supplementary social services, particularly secondary education and hospital facilities. The main political function of the commune is to supervise and implement the political and administrative policies of the Government and to strengthen the ideological and political basis of the rural society. The communes perform certain other functions, such as military training, control of the movement of population and the collection of Government taxes. The next higher level of State Government (the county) may maintain certain offices in a commune like a police station or an office of the county's grain department or a tax collection office, but these are largely supervised by the commune and some are being absorbed by the commune. Thus, while in its political role the commune is responsible for implementing governmental policy at the local level, its economic role is to provide leadership, guidance and assistance for agricultural and rural development through production planning, provision of essential inputs, the diversification of the rural economy and provision of certain social services. The extent to which a commune can perform these economic functions effectively will depend largely on its initial success in mobilising resources, either through brigades and teams or through its own projects and enterprises.

Thus the system of communes, while allowing smaller self-contained groups to plan, manage and share agricultural production through production teams and thus retaining some element of material incentives, provides for two supplementary levels of collectivisation and leadership, at which larger projects can be undertaken, supplementary resources can be generated and certain essential services provided for the benefit of members of the commune.

Another striking feature of the system of communes is the extent of decentralisation and autonomy it enjoys in the performance of its essential functions. Within the overall political framework and national policy on the use of national resources or the pattern of rural institutions, the communes have a very wide measure of autonomy for a whole range of economic and developmental functions. The commune and its constituent units are free to decide the best use of their land, water and human resources and how to distribute, save or invest their income. As explained later in this chapter, since taxation is fixed in absolute terms a commune retains the bulk of its additional income for its own consumption or investment. Even in the case of production planning, which is geared to certain national targets and quotas, the commune has in practice a great deal of flexibility in altering or exceeding the quotas. Production targets and quotas, while involving considerable discussion and negotiations, are essentially guidelines with a great deal of flexibility.

All the members of a commune form a People's Assembly which elects a People's Council consisting of 100 to 120 representatives. The Council in turn elects a Revolutionary Committee of ten to twenty-five members which performs day-to-day managerial and supervisory functions. In addition to this structure there is a Party Committee at the commune level elected by all the Party members in the commune. The first Secretary of the Party is in some communes also the Chairman of the Revolutionary Committee and other party officials may also be elected as members of the Revolutionary Committee with responsibility for certain specific activities. The Chairman is generally assisted by one or more Vice-Chairmen who generally look after the day-to-day operations of the commune. Other members of the Revolutionary Committee are responsible for one or more sub-sectors or specific activities. The mechanism of elections and the extent to which they are influenced by the party varies from place to place.

There are similar revolutionary committees at the brigade level elected by the members of the brigade and headed by a chairman and a vice-chairman. The structure is less formal at the production-team level but there is generally a head of the team and an accountant and four or five other team officials. With the exception of very few officials at the commune level who receive salaries, all other local officials are paid by local units and have to undertake part-time physical labour to earn their income. In practice, unlike local officials in other developing countries, it is difficult to distinguish them from the rest by their clothes or general appearance.

HOW THE SYSTEM WORKS

In the early stages of collective ownership of land, the first important factor in the Chinese approach to rural development was its ability to mobilise the unemployed and underemployed labour force, for improving the land, building dykes and dams, digging irrigation channels, constructing roads and simply cultivating the land more intensively.

In most other developing countries of Asia, available man-power in the rural areas cannot be fully utilised, at least partly, because of the pattern of land-ownership. A large portion of the rural population in these countries does not have enough land to absorb fully the time of the owners and their family members. If a sufficiently large area is collectively owned, it can not only absorb more labour per unit of land for more intensive cultivation, but it can utilise a considerable proportion of the surplus or seasonally unemployed labour for a wide variety of labour-intensive work, like land improvement, flood control and irrigation projects. The alternative of undertaking Government-financed public works to absorb some of the surplus labour and create some rural infrastructure has also been successfully tried in some other countries but, in the final analysis, the economic viability of these activities will depend on the conversion of the surplus labour into an economic surplus and that, in turn, will depend on the surplus value produced by this labour force over and above their own consumption. At a subsistence level, a worker is seldom willing to put in more work than is justified by his money wages unless he is working to improve his own land or future prospects. Thus the only way in which unemployed rural labour can be utilised to create a surplus for the benefit of rural areas is to organise it in such a way as to give it not only subsistence wages but a stake in improving the land and water resources. Then for a certain period of time, they would be prepared to create a 'surplus'. Even from an engineering point of view, collective ownership or close co-operation between all the owners is necessary before any sizeable irrigation or flood-control programme can be undertaken.

China's success in utilising the surplus labour force available in the rural areas was greatly facilitated by its policy of collectivisation and that success in turn created the impetus and the resources for the next stage in China's rural programme. No one can travel through the Chinese countryside without observing countless examples of labour-intensive works and being told with a marked sense of pride that these were built by the commune's own members.

The *second* important factor in the success of the Chinese commune is its ability to diversify the rural economy, first within the agricultural sector, to forestry, fisheries and livestock, and then to small industries, based on local raw materials or tools producing machinery and other inputs for agriculture.

A rapid and sustained increase in agricultural productivity and agricultural production is the first important objective of rural development but by itself it will not ensure a continuous improvement in living standards, particularly in countries with limited land resources. A gradual but continuous diversification of the rural economy is necessary not only for absorbing additions to the rural labour force but also to generate additional incomes for the rural population.

The process of diversification is initiated and strengthened at all levels. Each individual member and the production teams undertake 'sideline activities' like poultry and pig breeding, or fruit and vegetable growing to supplement their income. Then the production brigades begin to plan and implement other projects, such as simple food processing, fish breeding or livestock farms, with financial contributions or labour participation from the production teams. Finally, the commune performs the key entrepreneurial role of identifying new industrial possibilities, examining market prospects and supplying investment funds and technical know-how for implementation. Almost every commune has several industrial units producing cement, sugar, rice and flour mills, milk powder, paper, fertilizer, garments, and invariably some form of agricultural machinery. They have specialised farms for horses, dairy cows, pigs and ducks and specialised teams to expand and exploit the forestry and fisheries resources of the commune.

On the average, about 10–15 per cent of the available workforce in most communes is now engaged in forestry, fisheries, animal husbandry and in small-scale industry but the income derived from these diversified activities is about 30–40 per cent of the total income (see Appendix B). In other words, the income per head derived from these activities is twice as high as that from agriculture. These higher incomes do not, of course, accrue to individuals employed in these activities but to the commune or the brigade. For most of these activities the communes do not import skilled labour from outside but train their own farmers by forming them into specialised teams, and often make their own machinery. In this way, they do not wait for Government or industrial entrepreneurs to bring industries to their areas; they develop these industries according to their own needs and priorities, train their own workers and keep most of the extra income that this process creates.

The system of pricing for different commodities also helps the shift to sideline occupations by making them relatively attractive, but only after the communes have met their quotas for low-price grains. Thus a commune must produce a certain quantity of grain for its own use and for the State quota[4] if it happens to be a surplus commune, but after that it can supplement its income rapidly by diversifying into other activities and investing a growing surplus. Without this extra income it would be difficult for China to sustain or improve the standard of living of a rural population that does not have more than 0.20 hectares of cultivable land per person living in the rural areas. This continuing diversification of economic activities can be regarded as the most important factor in tackling the problem of rural employment. It absorbs the internal additions to the labour force and workers rendered potentially surplus by increasing productivity in agriculture. At the same time, it permits a gradual structural change in the rural economy that is in line with the factor endowment of China, i.e. a surplus of labour in relation to financial capital, and promotes step-by-step technological change. The resultant pattern, based on more appropriate technology, also helps to avoid many of the familiar environmental problems of today and leads to a better use of scarce resources such as energy, water and other materials.

The *third* important feature of the system is its progress in improving the knowledge and skills of the rural population. The longer-term success of efforts to achieve agricultural development does not depend so much on raising output per acre but on raising output per man and that in turn depends partly on his knowledge and partly on his access to capital, essential inputs and equipment. In the United States and Europe, output per man has increased much faster than output per acre, following a rapid transfer of population from the agricultural to non-agricultural sector and a substantial increase in the supply of capital and equipment. But in most developing countries of Asia and Africa, with 50, 60 or even 80 per cent of the population dependent on agriculture and with limited possibilities of shifting population to urban areas or non-agricultural sectors, salvation lies in using manpower within the agricultural sector and in gradually increasing productivity. Since there is no way in which all the farmers and rural workers can be educated, trained and equipped for higher productivity in a short period of time, they have to be organised and utilised initially in labour-intensive works already mentioned, but before long efforts must be made to improve their knowledge and skill and provide them with more modern inputs and equipment.

The system of rural education and training in China is geared to educating and training the rural population for work within the commune. This is very different from that in most other developing countries where the aim of education is considered to be white-collar jobs in the cities. The overriding impetus for the retention of skilled and educated population within the commune is, of course, provided by the political system which rewards mental and manual work about equally, emphasises manual work for everyone[5] and does not allow free mobility of labour between cities and rural areas. However, the collective system of ownership also permits the ready diffusion of knowledge in each unit of rural organisation on a uniform basis. As a result, the general level of technology tends to rise to the best available within a commune or brigade.

The *fourth* noteworthy feature of the system is its capacity for equitable distribution of incomes, thus ensuring that the benefits of larger production do not accrue to only a few members and that there is no re-emergence of a propertied class structure in the society. Because of the communal ownership of land and other assets, the bulk of a peasant's income is related mainly to the work done for collective production. Different kinds of activities earn 'work points' and each person gets wages, in kind and in cash, according to total work points earned in a month or a year. The rate at which work points are paid for is determined by dividing total net income of the production team or brigade (if that is the accounting unit) by the total number of work points. Thus, the income of a member depends partly on the number of work points earned but partly on the value of the work points as reflected in the results of the collective effort.

The system of work points is, in effect, a piece-rate system although in Chinese it is called 'bao-gong' or 'guaranteed work' system. Another system adopted initially by Tachai Production Brigade is less formal. Under this system, work points are not allotted for different items of work, but each member gives a subjective evaluation of his or her contribution at a public meeting about once a year. In general, the daily or monthly income received by different members under the Tachai system tends to be more equal than that under the *bao-gong* system in which the strongest or the best worker may receive twice as much as the older or weaker workers. Each commune is allowed to decide its own system of income distribution and in general support for the Tachai system is sought on grounds of political and ideological superiority, but in practice many households with old and weak workers have also supported the Tachai system since it can get them relatively higher wages.[6]

Almost every member earns, in addition to the income received from the collective, some private income from sales of produce from the private plot or other private endeavours like cutting and selling grass or wood from wastelands. This income varies enormously. In prosperous communes, when collective income is 150–60 Yuan per capita per year, a private income of, say, 30–40 Yuan is about 20 per cent of total income. But the same private income will constitute a larger proportion of a collective income of say 100–20 Yuan. In China, income from private plots whose total area does not exceed 5 per cent of the total cultivable area is often about 20 per cent more. This fact has sometimes encouraged some observers to suggest that private plots in China are more productive, which is not entirely true. The difference is essentially due to China's pricing policy in respect of grains and other products like meat, fruits and vegetables. A large portion of the collective land is used for producing food grains, whose prices are kept low as a matter of policy both for the issue of rations to members and for the State quota. (But quantities given to the State above the quota are priced 40–50 per cent higher.) Private plots are used mainly for poultry and pigs and for fruit and vegetables which fetch relatively higher prices, again as a matter of policy, at the local co-operative store or the village fairs. The most profitable item is pig raising. Private pig-breeding is encouraged, partly because it is a good source of organic manure, but also because veterinary science and practice in China is not yet fully developed to make collective hog-raising more profitable.

In the past twenty-five years from 1950 to 1975, the average per capita income in rural China has increased threefold from ¥50–60 in 1950–2 to about ¥160–70 in 1974–5. Since prices in China have remained practically unchanged over this period, the increase is real and not nominal. In more prosperous communes, the average income has reached ¥200. Since both husband and wife and their unmarried children work as a part of the same household, family income in practice is four to five times the per capita income. Converted into dollars, a yearly family income of ¥800–900 a year amounts to about $38–40 a month, but a comparison in terms of international exchange rates is meaningless. First of all, basic rations of grains, sugar, edible oils and fuel issued to every member cost only ¥10–12 ($5–6) a month. There is no rent, because commune members generally own their house. (New houses built by parents for their newly-married children require some investment for the purchase of materials which comes out of savings.) Education is free; medical services are paid for at a nominal rate of ¥1 a year. Different communes or brigades have also started providing many other community services free, like haircuts, nurseries for children, running water and community radio-receiving sets. Thus, in communes where average incomes are still in the range of ¥100–20 a year, rations issued in kind constitute 60–70 per cent of total income to be distributed, but in communes with higher incomes the cash portion is now 50 per cent or more and permits the family to buy, in addition to clothing and thermos flasks, other items of consumption such as bicycles, radios and watches.[7]

The manner in which the gross income of many typical production teams or brigades was distributed in 1974–5 is shown in the following table:

		%
Production expenses	(including seed fertilizer, organic manure, pesticide, machinery repair)	25–35
Social welfare fund	(education, medicine, casts and welfare subsidy for poor members)	2–3
State tax	(fixed in absolute terms)	3–5
Public accumulation Fund	(purchase of fixed assets and equipment and grain reserves)	10–15
Distributed to members		40–60[8]

The State's share of farm output in the form of a tax is fixed in absolute terms and, since farm output has been rising, farm taxation as a proportion of total output has declined from about 12 per cent in the 1950s to about 5 per cent in the 1970s. In some areas it is only 3 or 4 per cent. In addition, the communes' quotas for various crops are purchased from them at fixed prices, and the prices of goods bought by them are also fixed and stable. There is thus no external mechanism which takes away a larger proportion of the surplus value created in the commune. At the same time, since only about 40–60 per cent of the total gross revenue of the commune is distributed among the commune members, there is an upper ceiling on personal consumption. Considering the tax and the contribution to social welfare and the public accumulation fund and some non-monetised investment for projects (manual labour cannot be paid for from the accumulation fund), the effective rate of capital formation would seem to be well over 25 per cent of the commune's 'gross domestic product'.

The proportion of income devoted to social welfare seems small because it does not include services in kind. Salaries of teachers, health workers and barbers are counted in terms of work points and included under 'distribution to members'.

There are, of course, wide variations. In prosperous communes, the production expenses per unit of land are higher and so are contributions to the capital accumulation fund used for buying machinery, financing industrial projects or capital works. Some communes also create a revolving fund in addition to a capital accumulation fund for investment activities that create less permanent assets like orchards or for meeting emergencies. There are differences in personal incomes between different communes depending on the area and fertility of land, and between the best worker and the less efficient worker within a commune. But 90–5 per cent of the rural population in China receives incomes within a narrow range in which the highest income is only about twice the average income and does not raise its recipient to a different class of living. Perhaps the remaining 5 per cent of the population is still below the lower limit of this range. It is, therefore, no exaggeration to state that the rural development of China has combined growth with more egalitarian income distribution and that its rural population is on the average much better off than their counterpart in most other

Chinese rural development strategy is based upon the maximised use of all available resources and technological know-how. But, more importantly, its success depends on the mass mobilisation of the masses in a genuine co-operative effort.

A festive picture of mass mobilisation for the construction of San Menshia Dam.

Agriculture in China is like gardening. With 800 million persons depending on 110 million hectares, every inch of cultivable land in high productivity areas is cultivated and very well looked after. This is an experimental field of Nuhan Agricultural Training Institute

The San Menshia Dam is a major project to curb the treacherous waters of the Yellow River. 7000 permanent workers, joined by innumerable volunteers, mastered nature with the help of sophisticated technological equipment and know-how.

A 'rubber dam' in Hsin Hua People's Commune – about 60 km. from Canton is a good example of technological adaptation. The dam is installed in Kua Chi Chan reservoir built in 1966 in one month by 10,000 workers, with 6 embankments to create a 7-kilometer-long lake and an inflatable rubber dam which can rise to 2.7 metres to regulate flood water and feed an irrigation channel to irrigate about 2,000 hectares. The rubber dam came from Shanghai and cost only 30,000 Yuan ($15,000).

A 10-h.p.w. tractor manufactured in Chih Ying Commune agricultural machinery workshop. An example of intermediate technology

Above: *simple rice thrashing-machine*

Below: *a simple gadget for sowing cereal seed. Both are manufactured locally in the commune's workshop. An example of simple technology.*

developing countries in Asia and Africa. Rural incomes in China have increased significantly and these higher incomes have been distributed evenly and do not conceal the wide differences between large and small landowners that prevail in many other countries. Egalitarianism in China is, in fact, very visible even within a single locality.

The *fifth* significant factor in the success of the system is its role in planning. The system of communes provides a very effective mechanism of local planning in accordance with the simple philosophy 'From the bottom up and from the top down'. The planning process begins in every commune after the middle of each year, based on a review of last year's performance and next year's work plans. The commune's proposals, which largely reflect the proposals of various brigades and teams based on their own needs and priorities and the best use of available manpower and financial resources, are sent to the county which, after discussions with the commune, passes on total production targets and demands for items such as fertilizer and machinery to the province, which in turn submits them to the Central Planning Commission. The National Plan formulated by the Planning Commission covers targets for at least twenty-two commodities (including the main agricultural commodities such as grains, cotton, sugar, oilseeds and tea) with quotas for different provinces. At the annual meeting with provincial representatives the adequacy of targets for all major crops such as grains, sugar, cotton, vegetable oils is reviewed, deficit provinces are asked to increase production and deficits and surpluses are adjusted. The adjusted provincial targets are then passed back to lower levels and there is a second round of meetings to firm up the plans. The whole exercise is governed by two important principles – 'leaving leeway', which implies the need for maximum flexibility in planning, and 'combat selfishness', which requires everyone to take into account the need of others.

The system of planning is markedly different from that followed in many other developing countries, where all targets are determined in a national plan and their achievement sought through a combination of large public investments in expensive irrigation and infrastructure projects and economic policies to influence private-sector decisions. In the case of agriculture, this means a system of support prices and subsidies plus extension services. This system has achieved some results but the benefits have largely accrued to large farmers who have better access to technology, fertilizers, seed and credit.

The primary merit of the Chinese system of planning is its emphasis on maximum exploitation of local resources for meeting local needs. Central planners can seldom identify all the potentialities for local development or the right order of priorities. If a way could be found to organise the population in administrative and political units, large enough for some purpose or small enough for other purposes, to undertake the primary responsibility for their own development, they would not only simplify the task of central planning but could also generate their own resources for moving from one stage of development to the next, on the basis of maximum self-reliance.

Finally, the transition from agricultural to rural development is not complete until the rural community has established effective links with higher political and administrative levels and in-tegrated its planning and development activities with national targets, goals and policies. This becomes increasingly important as a rural community moves into the more advanced stages of agricultural and rural development. Requirements of inputs have to be co-ordinated at the provincial and national levels and surpluses and deficiencies have to be absorbed or provided for. The Chinese commune, while fairly autonomous and de-centralised in questions of land-use, relative priority of locally financed projects and distribution of the income generated by it, is on the whole well integrated in the processes of planning at the county, provincial and national levels. It also constitutes an important rung of the administrative and political hierarchy of the country to bring about perhaps the most important element in rural development – organisation. This does not mean that China has resolved all the inherent conflict between central planning and local initiative, but in practice the system does work.

The main thrust of the Chinese system is not merely on sending civil servants to rural areas 'to do things' for the people, as in most other countries, but in creating a system which the people and their local leaders organise and mobilise themselves in order to utilise their own resources and thus meet their own basic needs. And because of the collective ownership of the means of production and the gradual nature of technical progress, the entire rural population is undergoing a fundamental economic and social change with limited disparities in the distribution of the extra income and the standards of living.

The system of people's communes has thus accomplished all the three essential requirements of rural development in China, namely diversifying the rural economy, thus enabling it to absorb the additional labour force and generate additional incomes for the entire population; providing essential social services and a rural infrastructure; and integrating the activities of the commune with national targets, priorities and policies through carefully devised linkages with higher political and administrative levels. In essence, the commune represents not only a synthesis between social and technical transformation of a rural society but the main institutional tool through which the transition from agriculture to rural development, towards the objective of a modernised countryside, has been achieved.

5

Achievements and Prospects

China's achievements and progress cannot be judged purely in terms of growth rates, tons of food produced or number of jobs provided. One must move quickly from these quantitative data to certain social indicators of progress reflected in income distribution, educational and health facilities and equality of opportunity. But it is of even greater significance to go beyond these economic and social indicators and capture the profound change that has created a 'new man' and brought him into harmonious relationship with himself and with other human beings. In China, human beings and not things are the centre of all activity.

But let us first start with economic indicators which are impressive enough by any standard.

In the twenty-five year period since the liberation in 1949 China has seen periods of rapid progress and also of decline in production. If the first three years of recovery are excluded, in the subsequent twenty-two years taken as a whole China, according to some recent estimates, has achieved an average yearly increase of 6 per cent in gross domestic product, 3.2 per cent in agriculture, 9.7 per cent in industry and about 4.2 per cent in per capita income.

These figures, particularly the estimated agricultural growth rate of 3.2 per cent, are somewhat higher than previous estimates of 2.5 per cent as the long-term growth rate of this sector, but even the lower estimate is well ahead of the average population growth of 2 per cent per annum (now estimated to be growing at 1.7 per cent or even lower).[1] Per capita income in real terms has more than doubled over this period and the share of industry and transport in total gross national product has risen from 20–25 per cent to 45–50 per cent. Very few developing countries have done so well for such a long period of time.

Table 5.1 Chinese growth rates (in 1957 prices) (%)

Period	Industry	Agriculture	GDP
1952–7	12.1	6.8	7.8
1957–65	7.2	1.2	3.7
1965–70	10.3	4.1	7.2
1970–4	11.1	1.9	6.1
1952–74	9.7	3.2	6.1

Source: Dwight H. Perkins, *The Central Features of China's Economic Development*, paper presented to a Research Conference on The Lessons of China's Development Experience, Puerto Rico, January 1976, sponsored by the Sub-Committee on Research on the Chinese Economy of the Joint Committee on Contemporary China.

One of the most important manifestations of China's progress is its success in feeding its large population – estimated at 800 million people in 1975. Total grain production has more than doubled between 1949 and 1975 – from 108 million tons to 285 million tons. Since the increase in population over this period has been about 50 per cent, from 550 million to over 800 million, the per capita availability of cereals has increased from 200 kg per annum to 300 kg per annum.[2] Partly because of a sustained increase in grain production and partly due to the equitable distribution of available food supply, the proportion of malnourished population in China is very small.[3] In addition, the Chinese have pursued an active food-security policy. Following Chairman Mao's instructions in 1966 to 'dig tunnels deep, store grain everywhere and never exercise hegemony', the Chinese have been building food stocks, partly through surplus production and partly from imports. In 1975, total Government-controlled food stocks in China were estimated at 40 million tons. This did not include the stocks held by the communes and the brigades to meet their own fluctuations in production. Most of the stocks at commune and brigade levels and the Government stocks held at county level out of the agricultural tax paid in kind, are stored in small round clay silos of 100–200 ton capacity, built with mud and straw, coated in lime and paint, with concrete floors and proper fumigation and temperature control. Grain can be kept in these clay silos for five to seven years at a much lower cost than in mechanised silos. At the county level, house-type godowns are used with varying degrees of mechanisation and are integrated with flour mills. The Chinese storage system, I was told, is based on four principles, 'self-reliance, minimising costs, eliminating losses and ingenious use of local materials'. The Chinese are not yet fully satisfied with the level of existing stocks, which are only about 15 per cent of their annual consumption; they would like to have even bigger stocks to guard against major calamities. 'China is a large country and even a 5 per cent shortfall in its production is a large proportion (20 per cent) of the world's annual trade in wheat and rice. China should not export its problems to other countries', I was told during my second visit to China in February 1973.

The *second* important, almost unprecedented achievement of China is its ability to solve its employment problem. This has been accomplished by distributing available land and other assets more equitably among the rural population and then creating rural institutions that will provide opportunities for every one to do something useful and participate first in agricultural improvement and then in the gradual diversification of the rural economy in order to absorb the unavoidable additions to the labour force. The movement of population from the rural to urban areas is strictly controlled and there is no familiar influx of rural workers into urban areas to earn higher wages. This policy, while harsh in its impact on many individuals, has kept the relative increase in urban population almost in line with total population growth. (In most other developing countries, the rate of urban population growth has been twice as large as that in total population.) The success of this policy is, of course, due not only to the physical control on the movement of population, enforced indirectly through a comprehensive rationing system in cities, but also to the continuing improvement in rural life itself, with opportunities for higher incomes and varied activities. Efforts have also been made to contain increments in urban wages in order to narrow the gap between urban and rural standards of living.

One of the most important factors in China's success in tackling its food and employment problems has been its effective population policy. China has already brought down the crude birthrate to less than thirty per 1000, which is much lower than the forty to fifty range in the majority of developing countries. With a crude death rate of twelve to thirteen per 1000, China's population is now growing at 1.7 and probably even a slower rate.[4] China has perhaps the most comprehensive population planning programme in the world, based partly on late marriages. Marriage is legally permitted at the age of eighteen for women and twenty-two for men, but prospective couples are encouraged to wait until their mid or late twenties. In addition there is a policy of birth spacing of four to five years and a 'Birth Plan' with a kind of collective but flexible decision-making to achieve a 'two child norm'. The programme is, of course, supported by a very efficient system of family-planning education and contraceptive materials.

Third, China has managed to avoid the problem of inflation by keeping the prices of basic necessities almost stable for the past twenty-five years. In August 1975 the prices of some necessities in Shanghai compared to those in 1950 were reported to be as follows:

	1950 (¥uan)	*1974* (¥uan)
Rice (50 kg)	17.63	16.40
Pork (½ kg)	0.80	0.98
White cloth (1 m)	0.28	0.28
Coal (50 kg)	2.86	2.50

Note: One ¥uan was equal to 0.40 dollars in 1950 and 0.56 dollars in 1974.

The slight decrease in the retail price of rice was brought about despite a rise in the basic purchase price paid to the communes since the Cultural Revolution. Prices in China are also unaffected by changes in world prices since all imports and exports are arranged by the Government which supplies or buys everything at fixed prices. Chinese exports and imports (6.3 and 7.4 billion dollars respectively in 1974) are, in any case, a very small proportion of their GNP (less than 10 per cent for total trade in 1974). The Chinese make a limited use of the price system by offering, for example, relatively higher prices for some cash crops or products of sideline occupations to encourage diversification, or by keeping the prices of mass-consumed 'luxuries' such as bicycles, radios or watches somewhat higher than the 'real' cost of production. This not only prevents the consumption of such goods from rising very fast but also provides a more acceptable form of taxation in collecting some extra revenue. But as a matter of overall policy, the Chinese rely on the planning system and not the price system to balance the demand and supply of various commodities and goods. 'The price system', I was told, 'is generally manipulated in other countries by the capitalists or by the middle men against the common consumer, the worker and the peasant. The impact of inflation is particularly heavy on the urban workers. Even if they resort to strikes to get higher wages they seldom get full compensation for inflation, and by the time they get some increase the inflation has eroded their real income again.'

And *finally*, and most significantly, because of the sustained increase in industrial and agricultural production and because of an equitable system of income distribution, China has managed to meet the basic needs of almost every Chinese. 'The days in which the majority of Chinese were without food and clothing have gone for ever,' I was told. 'There is no Chinese man or woman today whose basic needs of food, clothing, housing, education and medicines are not met.' How many other countries of Asia, Africa and Latin America can make this claim for the foreseeable future?

The 'five guarantees' (Wu Bao Hu) for those who cannot work include food, clothing, shelter, education and a decent burial, but health has gradually been added to the list unofficially because production teams have assumed responsibility for medical expenses of their members. The guarantee of a decent burial is of considerable psychological importance after the bitter memories of so many people dying on the roadside before liberation. The Chinese system of five guarantees is a modest but remarkable system of social welfare for a country at China's stage of development and is implemented largely by local institutions to whom the recipient belongs, through their own limited resources. In practice, everyone who is fit to work has to work to meet his or her basic needs and the total family income is now, on the average, larger than necessary to pay for food and minimum clothing. There is consequently a visible improvement in the standard of housing and in the acquisition of such items as thermos flasks, bicycles, radios, watches and some simple items of furniture. The standard of housing is poor and drab by Western standards, but no one sleeps on the pavements or in the open. A typical family of five will have a two-room flat in the city or a two-room house in the rural areas, with a norm of 4.5 square metre per person. Single people generally live in dormitories or share houses. In every commune, 200–300 new houses are being built every year with material provided by the commune and labour provided by the family and volunteers.

SOCIAL INDICATORS

The expansion of education and health facilities in rural China has been extremely rapid. It can be readily seen from the data presented in Appendix B that each commune with an average population of 20,000 to 25,000 has twenty to twenty-five primary schools, which works out to about one school for 100 children of ages five to eleven, assuming 10 per cent of the population to be in that age group. Secondary schooling is now being provided in rural areas with an expanding number of junior and senior middle schools. More promising students go to higher education institutions and technical schools, provided their political and ideological orientation and motivation is considered to be positive.

China's health policy is squarely based on preventive medicine and environmental hygiene. The Chinese seldom drink unboiled water and therefore the incidence of water-borne diseases is relatively low. They almost never walk barefoot (and this applies to barefoot doctors) and thus minimise the risk of insectborne infections. Emphasis on sanitation and health education is widespread and visible. When it comes to curative medicines, the Chinese have clearly recognised that extensive and comprehensive coverage for everyone can be achieved only by sacrificing excellence and lowering the standard of buildings and other physical facilities. This in turn has led to the well-known programme of barefoot doctors whose total number is now over one and a half million. About two-thirds of the total budget on medicine is spent in rural areas and every commune has a hospital with twenty to fifty beds or at least a clinic. Several brigades have started establishing clinics and most have a few barefoot doctors, who are essentially trained peasants or educated youths who can look after minor ailments through a combination of traditional and modern medicine. In most communes, every adult member pays a nominal fee of 1 or 2 Yuan per year to receive the required medical facilities, but hospitalisation involves some extra expenditure which is often met, at least partially, by the team, brigade or the commune. Like any other country, China still faces many problems in the public-health sector but there is hardly an illness or an accident that goes untreated in China today. Of greater significance is the improvement in the general health of the people. Because of better nutrition and improved sanitation, the incidence of sickness has gone down considerably.

China's approach to improve personal consumption and facilities is very pragmatic and often ingenious. For example, one production brigade, faced with surplus milk in the absence of a milk-powder plant or ready commercial demand, quickly set up arrangements to convert it into ice-cream for free distribution to members of the brigade. Similarly, with increased emphasis on recreation and visits to places of historic or scenic interest, many co-operative stores began to rent cameras for a few cents a day. 'Most people seldom use their cameras more than once or twice a year. Hiring a camera is better and cheaper than owning one,' I was told by my Chinese hosts. Facilities and cultural activities now being expanded in many rural areas include community radio and broadcasts, extended to farms and factories through loudspeakers, regular film shows, free running water and co-operative stores with a variety of consumer goods. In short, rural life in all parts of China is improving gradually but visibly.

Perhaps one of the most important social changes in China is the transformation in the status of women. They are no longer subservient to a father, brother or husband. They have increasing opportunities for work and responsibility, particularly in techni-cal activities including industry and in education, health and sanitation. Almost all women have been integrated into the workforce and an impressive number have risen to positions of responsibility and leadership. In the Shanghai area, for example, of the 120,000 young cadres who have joined the ranks of the Communist Party since 1968, at least one-quarter are women. The average wages received by women workers are still lower than those received by men because their work is supposed to be lighter, but the Chinese women are much closer in equality with men than their counterparts in most other developing countries.

THE IDEOLOGICAL FRAMEWORK

But as already mentioned, increments in GDP, per capita income and food supply, or improvements in health and education facilities do not truly reflect China's real achievements. These are much more qualitative and are symbolised in the 'new man'[5] in China and in the new political and social structure in which he works and lives with others.

Since the liberation in 1949 every Chinese has a greater sense of security of life and sustenance. He is no longer afraid of natural calamities or famines. He has a greater sense of dignity as regards his work and profession, his family and working environment. Manual or ordinary work is no longer considered inferior. He can marry and raise a family according to his own choice and a Chinese is proud to be a Chinese. There is also a much greater equality of opportunity and reward and he is no longer exploited by the landlord or the official. He has a fuller sense of participation in economic activities and in making decisions that affect his life.

But how has all this come about? What is the nature and magnitude of the social change that has pervaded China since 1949?

The liberation of 1949, coming as the culmination of a prolonged struggle and much turmoil, created the preconditions for a new society based on socialist ideology. The main ingredients of this ideology, seldom clearly defined, nevertheless include the following:

(*a*) a preference for collective over individual gain, reward and welfare;

(*b*) the creation of a classless society which can eliminate or minimise all form of exploitation;

(*c*) the gradual evolution of a self-reliant society in which every village, commune, province and ultimately the whole nation develops its own resources to meet its needs on a basis of equality and without recreating different classes.

Each of these elements is based on a profound ideological concept which has to be spelled out at different times in more specific terms in relation to the particular situation, conflict or contradiction. Each of these elements then requires the support of appropriate structures and policies which, in turn, reshape the concept itself. It is this continuous interaction between the concepts, the structure and actual policies that has created the organic and dynamic society we see in China today.

The concept of *collective welfare* in preference to individual gain, for example, starts at the family level and moves to the village, county, provincial or national level for different purposes, and requires collective (as distinguished from Government or State) ownership and a system of joint decision-making and everyone's participation in the solution of the problems. But how large should the units of collective ownership be, how flexible the power of decision-making, how complete the sense of participation? These questions were not answered by the Chinese overnight. The solutions were evolved and are still evolving through experience and mistakes, as brought out in the preceding chapters. The cultivation of land, for example, is now in effect collectivised at the production-team level, but other assets such as small factories or agricultural machinery at the brigade or commune level. This provides material incentives for harder work, but if these incentives go too far and lead to greed and dishonesty, there is fear of punishment by being classified as a 'bad element'. There are also moral pressures generated by the system which require self-discipline and for the deviationist there is a kind of group supervision lurking all the time in the background.

Again, the concept of a *classless society* is not confined to equalisation of property or income. Classes can emerge in many different ways and exploitation of one class by another can take many different forms. In China, the Cultural Revolution of 1966 – 7 was at least partly designed to prevent the re-emergence of the class system through the bureaucracy which, after losing touch with the masses, began to consider itself superior and devoted increasing attention to improving its personal standard of living.[6] This continuous struggle to suppress selfishness and preserve a classless society requires different kinds of policies, campaigns and political movements at difference stages. There is no limit, for example, on the purchase of consumer goods or on the improvement of living standards, but a pattern of consumption that raises one group to a 'higher class' is not permitted. That is why the Chinese have gone from the bicycle to the aeroplane, skipping the automobile. The aeroplane, although still available to a few, is a means of public transport; television sets can become a mass-consumed luxury. But a car cannot, since the Chinese cannot afford to have 200 million cars (one per family of four or five). Again, attempts to build a classless society which will end exploitation implies, paradoxically, that in practice there is always an actual or potential class against which the masses are waging a struggle to protect the objective of socialism.

The principle of *self-reliance*, similarly, does not mean autarky or total self-sufficiency. All it means is that one should produce whatever one can oneself at the level of the family, village, commune, province or nation, and not depend on others. Again, this concept is promoted and supported by the collective structure and leads to a much better use of the country's physical and human resources. Sometimes it means excessive zeal and relatively inefficient production (like the backyard furnaces to produce steel in the late 1950s) but the Chinese have quickly learned from their mistakes. Their notion of 'size' for different activities has been very flexible and, when the concept of self-reliance did not fit into a given size, the size was adjusted to provide for greater economic and technical efficiency.

Material incentives are not only present but fairly strong in China. Without a visible and sustained improvement in the material situation of the average Chinese, the system would not have evolved as successfully as it has. But material incentives are not the primary motivation in China. They are circumscribed by and subservient to the three elements of ideology referred to above. Even more important, the manner in which these three elements have evolved in China has created a new, almost religious zeal and fervour in support of the ideology. The result is the emergence of a man who is not selfish, who works hard in return for basic necessities, and who from a social, ethical and moral point of view is a good human being. Organised crime or for that matter serious individual crime is extremely rare in China. The country is almost free of other common social evils of the contemporary world, such as prostitution, gambling, smuggling and drug addiction. It is a truly phenomenal social transformation for one-fifth of mankind.

Thus China's pursuit of material objectives is not an end in itself but a means to create a collective, classless and self-reliant society. In this sense, China's socialism is basically 'humanistic' in its approach and based on a positive moral and ethical code based on collective welfare and responsibility. China's concept of 'humanism', it must be emphasised, is not identical with the Western concept in which every individual's freedom and rights have to be respected irrespective of their impact on social or egalitarian objectives. In China, the concept of humanism is secondary to that of socialism. Those who oppose socialism or the revolution are enemies of the people and must be maligned or reformed. But within the framework of socialism, the individual must acquire an identity and a personality which must grow as a part of a collective. The collective which may be a production team, a brigade, a commune, a factory, a city or a nation is an association of individuals and exists for his welfare and development. As long as he is ready to carry out his responsibility as a member of this association his basic needs will be met, he will have dignity and self-respect and will have the opportunity to participate in the affairs and management of the collective. This concept of the individual as a part of the collective creates a new value system which postulates on the basic equality of man. It generates a new spirit of co-operation among people which transcends purely material rewards and leads to a sense of achievement and fulfilment which is not only related to a material standard of living but comes from shared austerity.

Is socialism in China fundamentally different from socialism in east Europe? Has Mao added some new non-material ideological elements to Marxism – Leninism? Or has he simply brought together certain moral and ethical principles of socialism which were scattered in Marx's writings but were not the central part of Marxian dialectic. When I put these questions to some Chinese teachers of Marxism – Leninism in China, their answers were as follows:

No. The principles of Marx, Lenin and Mao are the same but in China, practice is closely tied to theory. Also Mao combined the needs and lessons of the Chinese Revolution with Marxist thinking. The main aim of socialism is to end exploitation but in the process, new and more subtle forms of exploitation develop. Mao therefore goes from material incentives to revolutionary spirit and back to material rewards. 'Continuing revolution' means from capitalism to democratic socialism, from there to full socialism and from there to Communism. In Communism, the principle of 'from each according to his ability, to each according to his need' is the guiding rule. China is still in the socialist stage and a long way off from the stage of Communism.

Marxism has been interpreted widely and differently by scholars and political thinkers but there is agreement on at least two points. First, that Marx's critique of the capitalistic system constitutes the hardcore of his entire thesis and, second, that he presented some philosophical concepts of socialism but not the blueprint of a socialist society. Beyond that, Marx's concepts of man, nature and society, his treatment of labour and its relationship with modes of organisation and production, the age-old problems inherent in the exercise of power and control, have generated considerable heat and much controversy.

Mao's approach to socialism is essentially based on the basic philosophical concepts of Marx, but he gave a clearly Chinese orientation to Marxian concepts and principles by relating them to Chinese history and interpreting the main issues in the context of the cultural and psychological circumstances of China. He also accepted and strengthened Lenin's emphasis on the international implications of the capitalistic system, his theory of continuing revolution and the role of the collective spirit.

In his famous essay 'On Contradiction', first written in August 1937 but revised for inclusion in his selected works,[7] Mao explains the Marxist world outlook of materialist dialectics:

Changes in society are due chiefly to the development of internal contradictions in society, that is, the contradiction between classes, and the contradiction between the old and the new; it is the development of these contradictions that pushes society forward and gives the impetus for suppression of the old society by the new. Does material dialectics exclude external causes? Not at all. It holds that external causes are the conditions of change and internal causes are the basis of change, and that external causes become operative through internal causes.

Mao also points out that the dialectical world outlook had emerged in ancient times both in China and in Europe but

ancient dialectics had a somewhat spontaneous and naïve character; in the social and historical conditions then prevailing, it was not yet able to form a theoretical system, hence it could not fully explain the world and was supplanted by metaphysics (in which things are seen as isolated, static and one-sided and in which motive force for change is external rather than internal). . . . It was not until Marx and Engels, the great protagonists of the proletarian movement, had synthesized the positive achievements in the history of human knowledge and, in particular, critically absorbed the rational elements of Hegelian dialects and created the great theory of dialectical and historical materialism that an unprecedented revolution occurred in the history of human knowledge. This theory was further developed by Lenin and Stalin. As soon as it spread to China, it wrought tremendous changes in the world of Chinese thought.

This dialectical world outlook teaches us primarily how to observe and analyse the movement of opposites in different things and on the basis of such analysis to indicate the methods for resolving contradictions. It is therefore most important for us to understand the laws of contradictions in a concrete way.

Mao then proceeds to explain at some length the important distinction between the universality and particularity of contradiction. Universal contradictions were illustrated by Lenin as 'Differential and integral in mathematics; action and reaction in mechanics; positive and negative in electricity in physics; the combination and dissociation of atoms in chemistry and the class struggle in social science'. But 'Every form of motion' Mao explains in this essay

Contains within itself its own particular contradiction. . . .

Every form of society, every form of ideology, has its own particular contradiction and particular essence . . .

Qualitatively different contradictions can only be resolved by qualitatively different methods. For example, the contradiction between the proletariat and the bourgeoisie is resolved by the method of socialist revolution; the contradiction between the great masses of the people and the feudal system is resolved by the method of democratic revolution; the contradiction between the colonies and imperialism is resolved by the method of national revolutionary war; the contradiction between the working class and the peasant class in socialist society is resolved by the method of collectivization and mechanization in agriculture; contradiction within the Communist Party is resolved by the method of criticism and self-criticism; the contradiction between society and nature is resolved by the method of developing the productive forces.

Mao also explains in this essay the principal contradiction and the principal aspect of a contradiction and the place of antagonism in contradiction. Mao's discourse on contradiction not only takes the Marxian concept of dialectics a step further but relates it to certain fundamental Chinese concepts. In fact, as Mao himself points out in this essay, the Chinese view of dialectics is almost 2000 years old. (The ancient Chinese saying 'things that oppose each other also complement each other' first appeared in Pan Ku's *History of the Earlier Han Dynasty* in the first century A.D.) This view of dialectics in turn springs from the Chinese philosophy of good and bad or right and wrong. According to the traditional Chinese philosophy, energy (chi) circulates through the universe under the control of forces called *yin* and *yang*, which correspond to the ebb and flow of any pair of opposing forces such as good and bad or light and dark. This explanation not only leads to many theories basic to the Chinese system of medicine and techniques like acupuncture (which serves to restore the natural rhythm of energy flow), but also provides the basis of the Chinese concept of dialectics. The world consists of units or elements but all the elements are contradictory and these opposing forces or 'contradictions' are built into everyone of them. Hence one cannot finally sort out positive/negative, active/ passive or good/bad. Each of these has the element of the other and nothing is perfect. One should not therefore condemn a person who has committed a crime. He is reformable. Similarly, a good person will not always be good. His negative side may emerge later. And ultimately, if the contradiction becomes widespread, then the whole system must undergo a total change, marginal reform or improvements would not be enough (as in class struggle). In a positive sense, the philosophy of 'walking on two legs' or that of combining traditional and modern technology, agriculture and industry or material and non-material incentives, springs from this view of dialectics: both have positive and negative elements. This is different from the more unilinear dialectics of the Western Marxist.[8]

Thus in philosophical terms, Mao has added many positive dimensions to Marxian dialectics – the philosophy of walking on two legs and the judicious use of the collective spirit. But in practical terms, China under Mao's leadership did not follow what is normally considered as the typical Marxist development model. It gave higher priority to agriculture and rural development over industry, and did not rush into heavy industry. Within agriculture, China adopted the system of communal ownership of land in which the rural population has a sense of belonging and participation and not of large state-owned collective farms in which the majority of workers are only wage earners and do not take part in deciding what to grow or how to increase productivity. The people's communes, as already explained in Chapter 4, are also built on the Chinese cultural tradition of living and working together.

Mao also succeeded in presenting a very different approach to the role of top political leadership. He emphasised the supremacy of political and ideological factors in all spheres of activity but the task of the political leadership was not conceived by him in terms of a centralised and tightly controlled political system. He evolved a decentralised system, with motivated and trained cadres providing leadership at all levels. At each level the main task of the cadres was to derive their ideas from the masses in a participatory process whose main purpose was to serve the interests of the masses. In other words he succeeded in transferring real political power to the poor masses. In a single-party system in a large country, the task of retaining and exercising this power for the benefit of masses is not easy, as is clear from the experience of the Cultural Revolution and periodical political strains that have been noticed in China. But the two basic objectives of socialism, viz. ending the direct or indirect exploitation of the masses, and evolving a self-reliant and participatory development and political framework, have at least so far remained intact. Mao also succeeded in generating a new kind of ideological fervour and non-material motivation to supplement the limited material rewards available to the population.

All the theoretical and philosophical elements of Mao's socialism and the main elements of China's ideology have yet to be clearly explained and articulated, but Mao's real achievement is his success in actually implementing a much bolder and bigger experiment in socialism and in the process discarding a great deal of 'conventional wisdom' from right and left.

FUTURE PROSPECTS

What are China's future prospects? Can the rate of agricultural and industrial growth achieved in the past twenty-six years be sustained? Is the system viable in the long run? Will it survive after Mao? These are questions that no one can answer with certainty but some possibilities and prospects can be outlined.

China's development policy is based on a long-range Perspective Plan which began in 1965 and covers the period up to the year 2000. The advent of the Cultural Revolution in 1966 probably prevented the release or public discussions of the plan but Premier Chou En-lai in his report to the Fourth National People's Congress – which is China's supreme political and legislative organ – explained its two main stages. The first stage (1965–80) 'is intended to build an independent and relatively comprehensive industrial and economic system' which will provide the basis for the second stage (1980–2000) in which 'the comprehensive modernisation of agriculture, industry, national defence and science and technology will be accomplished'. Premier Chou En-lai also announced a New Ten Year Plan for the period 1975–85 to bridge the end of Stage One and the beginning of Stage Two. The objectives of basic mechanisation of agriculture by 1980 and the construction of large fertilizer plants which flow from this plan have been mentioned in the preceding chapters.

Judging by the progress achieved in implementing the first stage of the long-range plan during the period 1965–75 and the realistic yet vigorous manner in which the implementation of the New Ten Year Plan (1975–85) has begun, the prospects for a continued expansion of agriculture and industry would seem to be fairly bright. In fact, if China succeeds in implementing its plans for the basic mechanisation of agriculture and the production of a much larger supply of chemical fertilizer, it could emerge as a major potential exporter of food. In practice, China would probably build up even larger stocks of food rather than become a regular food exporter, but even its potential capacity for sizeable food exports could be of considerable political and economic significance for other developing countries in an era of chronic food shortages. In 1975 almost 80 per cent of the world's grain exports were provided by only two countries (the United States and Canada). Any major climatic setback in North America can have a disastrous impact on the world food situation. The prospects of China's emergence even as an occasional exporter of food should be considered a positive element in this situation.

China's longer-term aim of comprehensive modernisation by the turn of this century still faces many uncertainties. China's initial technological drive was launched in the late 1950s and aimed at rapid industrialisation in the countryside, mainly through metallurgical industries and supported by heavy industries in the urban sectors. This programme did not get very far, partly because the aims were unrelated to the level of development and the resultant demand in the country and partly because two other complementary sectors – energy and transport – were neglected. Many of the small-scale metallurgical industries in the countryside were therefore closed down in 1961. But on the basis of that experience, China has now evolved a technology policy which seems much more viable. It is based on a combination of large, medium and small-scale industries. The large-scale industries will use the latest technology, while the medium and small-scale industries are designed to support the process of rural industrialisation, emphasising indigenous or intermediate technology and the intensive use of labour and are geared to the requirements of agricultural production or the consumption needs of the rural population.

The focal point for rural industrialisation is the county level, where a large proportion of agricultural inputs are produced (cement, chemical fertilizer, iron and steel, machinery and energy), facilities for farm machinery repair and manufacture created, and light consumer goods and agricultural processing industries set up. For each of these industries, efforts are made to develop a kind of network, in which the communes and brigades take up the simpler components or units. In 1975 about 60 per cent of chemical fertilizer, 50 per cent of all cement and two-thirds of all tractors were manufactured in small-scale industries located in the rural areas, i.e. county and below. While some of these industries, such as chemical fertilizer and sophisticated agricultural machinery, are being supplemented by the modern sector, a solid base of rural industrialisation, which can absorb a sizeable slice of manpower and generate its own surplus for further expansion, has already been laid.

In the modern industrial sector, China reached a certain technological plateau in the early 1970s for certain sub-sectors, requiring more sophisticated and advanced technology, such as specialised steel, large-scale petro-chemical industries, electronics, aeronautics and advanced communications. Efforts are now being made to import advanced technology and machinery for these sub-sectors and these are partly reflected in the sharp increase in China's imports – from $4975 million in 1973 to $7410 million in 1974.[9] The discovery of large petroleum deposits in the Taching oilfields and the recent modernisation of pipeline and port facilities have improved the prospects for a substantial expansion of industries based on petroleum and energy. China's petroleum resources and its judicious use of those resources could enable her to become a major petroleum exporter if, as a matter of policy, the country wanted to export it rather than conserve it for its own future use.

But access to advanced technology and energy resources is only one of the obstacles to comprehensive modernisation. The whole question of industrial relations and the conflict between political and technological factors and between the requirements of rapid modernisation and socialist relations of production is bound to re-emerge. Mao has always recognised that the question of 'management' is the most important problem after 'ownership'. In his *Notes on Political Economy*, written in 1960, he suggested several steps to close the gap between the worker and the management – 'leadership by the Party and combining centralized leadership with mass movements; integration of workers and technicians; participation of cadres in manual labour, participation of workers in management – continuous change of unreasonable codes and conventions'.[10] After the Cultural Revolution, organised workers have acquired a greater role but sometimes this pattern does not meet the full requirements of advanced technology and modernisation. The new Chinese Constitution approved by the Fourth National People's Congress has also approved 'the right to strike' as one of the Chinese people's basic liberties, but this means a 'strike for socialism', i.e. workers' right to assert themselves in management, rather than a 'strike for capitalism', i.e. for greater financial rewards which is looked down upon. In early 1976 the focus of the political debate was in favour of according higher priority to socialist transition over the requirements of technology and modernisation but this will be an unending see-saw in China's future development policy.

Another sector in which China has a long way to go is the transport system. Even in the mid-1970s the bulk of rural transport in China was manual or animal-drawn involving tremendous physical strain for the population. Any visitor going from a rural to an urban area in any part of China can observe a stream of people, bullocks, mules and donkeys carrying stones, lime, timber, coal, fertilizer, grain, vegetables, fruit and a variety of other products in hand-carts, donkey-carts, bullock-carts, mule-carts and, now increasingly, in trucks and tractors. The mechanisation of transport has started but it will take a long time before Chinese transport is fully mechanised.

China has also to seek a more effective solution for the problem of regional disparities. Because of collective ownership of land and other means of production, the disparity in personal incomes within an area or a region has been considerably narrowed, but the problem of income disparity between regions still remains, particularly for remote areas with poor land and natural resources. The present system aiming at self-reliance for each region does not permit sizeable transfer of resources from one region to the other. There are also cultural differences which inhibit any large-scale infusion of technical and managerial skills.[11]

These problems and obstacles are not insurmountable and China has already demonstrated its capacity to overcome problems and to learn from its mistakes. China has already built a solid base of agricultural and industrial production; it is now embarking on more rapid technological development both in agriculture and industry; it has the potential to develop an export surplus in two critical commodities – food grains and petroleum. All these factors taken together would lend considerable weight to the Chinese expectations that they will catch up with the West in terms of industrial and agricultural productivity and technological progress by the turn of this century (even if the apparent gap between per capita incomes remains large). If they do China will have achieved, in a period of fifty years, a level of development which the Western countries reached in 150–200 years and Japan in seventy to eighty years. And in many ways China's progress will be more commendable because it will not be based on the exploitation of any colonial territories. It will not involve the wasteful use of scarce natural resources and hopefully will not lead to inequalities in income and economic opportunities for different segments of society.

But just as the past quarter century of modern China has not been without difficulties, the next quarter century will not be entirely smooth. China is still a developing country with a standard of living that is just rising above the subsistence level for the majority of its population. It will require a tremendous effort to maintain the tempo of progress within an egalitarian framework. And no one can really predict the many new problems which the next phase of China's development will inevitably create. These might in part arise from the unavoidable transition from a 'subsistence, basic needs type' economy to a developed one in which a wide range of consumer goods are needed and can be produced. Can China continue to keep personal consumption down to a modest level after everyone's basic needs are met? Can they cope with a resurgence of young people who ask for more education and greater opportunities for cultural and intellectual freedom? Can they keep the ideological fervour at the same pitch for the next twenty to twenty-five years to provide the main motivation for preserving a self-reliant and collective society?

Only time will answer these questions and on these answers will depend not only China's future but the course of a new historical pattern in which, after two centuries of technological and materialistic progress, man is, for the first time, seeking a more social and moral basis for human progress.

Postscript: China after Mao

Chairman Mao Tse-tung died on 9 September 1976, only a few months after Premier Chou En-lai's death. These two outstanding leaders led the Chinese people for almost fifty years – first through the revolutionary struggle from 1926 to 1949 and then in building a new and self-reliant China. Their departure within the same year is a traumatic event in the history of China and 'China after Mao' will become a major subject worthy of careful study for many years to come.

The immediate concern is naturally centred on the inevitable problems of succession and on China's international relations, but beyond that China's future development and economic policy will be watched carefully. The key question underlying the current debate about moderate versus radical policy or conservative versus revolutionary policy is undoubtedly the future of Mao's political philosophy and the survival of the Chinese system as developed under Mao's charismatic leadership.

It is perhaps too early to find any conclusive evidence or indicators on which to base any predictions about China's future but my own personal assessment is that Mao's political philosophy will continue to guide China's destiny, and China's longer-term prospects discussed earlier in this chapter will not be adversely affected by Mao's death.

The problems facing the new Chinese leaders are numerous and complex and initial indications point to a shift towards 'moderate' policies. But the terms 'moderate' and 'radical' have peculiarly Chinese meanings. In a fundamental sense the difference between the two approaches is perhaps not much greater than that between Conservative and Labour policies in Britain or between the Republican and Democratic policies in the United States.

A 'radical' approach in China implies greater emphasis on moral incentives and equality of incomes rather than higher salaries and greater opportunities for personal consumption or advancement. It also calls for greater emphasis on self-reliance and indigenous technology to reduce dependence on imports from other areas within the country and from other countries.

The so-called 'moderate' approach favours selective relaxation of material incentives, greater scope for specialisation and larger trade with other countries to speed up the process of industrialisation and modernisation. It would also allow greater choice to students to choose their fields of study or careers.

There is a great deal of truth in both the viewpoints and the real choice is not between one or the other approach but the precise mixture at a given point of time. The conflict between the two approaches is not new and has been faced and resolved in the past. The Cultural Revolution of 1966–8 was, of course, a major shift towards the 'radical' approach as a reaction to gradual relaxation in favour of 'moderate' policies in the early 1960s.

Mao's death in 1976 coincided with a phase of Chinese development in which the process of mechanisation and modernisation was being strengthened. This in turn required a larger number of research workers and trained technicians and greater emphasis on career planning and material incentives. It also implied somewhat larger dependence on the import of sophisticated equipment and technology. A debate about the full implications of this phase of development had in fact started before Mao's death with many difficult questions coming to the forefront. Can modern industry be developed without allowing the gap between the town and the country to widen again? Can the required expertise and skilled manpower be developed without strengthening material incentives and encouraging greater specialisation? Can imports from other countries be increased without eroding the principle of self-reliance?

In the absence of Mao's personal charisma, his strong commitment to ideological motivation and his political ability to seek sacrifices from the population, the new leaders of China may have to rely a little more on material incentives and technical considerations to seek their immediate objectives. This shift to moderate policies will naturally be resisted by those who are strongly opposed to any dilution of the ideological approach. There will be considerable controversy in the coming years over specific issues of policy and over the approach as a whole.

Whether or not this controversy will undermine the system as a whole will depend very much on the ability of the leadership to maintain the right balance between the two approaches.

The manner in which the new Chinese leaders are seeking to achieve this balance is at least partly illustrated by the Second Agricultural Conference on 'Learning from Tachai' held in December 1976. The Conference was attended by 5000 delegates from all parts of the country including the top party leadership.[12] Its declared purpose was to consolidate the lessons of the first Agricultural Conference held in October 1975 since these had been distorted by the 'gang of four'. The convening of a national conference on agriculture, within two months of the change in national leadership, however, also underlines the fact that China intends to push for modern industry without minimising the importance of rural development. More than 80 per cent of China's population still live in rural areas and the basic needs for food, clothing and simple consumer goods can be met only through continued progress in agriculture and rural industries.

But within this re-emphasis on agriculture, the conference promised more State assistance to supplement the self-help programmes of the rural population. There have also been reports of wage increases for industrial workers and greater opportunities for technical education.

These shifts towards moderate policies can, of course, go too far if they recreate major differences in life styles or upset the classless nature of the Chinese society. But it would be naïve to assume that these shifts already imply a basic change in the Chinese system or the end of Mao's political philosophy. At the same time, future efforts of the Chinese leaders to restore the 'balance' will require continued reliance on Mao's teachings presented under new ideological labels or special campaigns which out-siders may not easily appreciate.

The survival and viability of the Chinese model of develop-ment after Mao is important not only for China but also for many other developing countries whose material resources are too limited to build consumer societies on the Western model.

Part II

MAIN LESSONS OF THE CHINESE EXPERIENCE

6

A Theoretical Framework for Rural Development

In the early 1950s, when concern with development economics first began, the concept of development was almost synonymous with economic growth. The most serious misconception of that time was the simplistic notion that economic development could be promoted simply by pushing up the investment ratio from 5 – 6 per cent of gross national product to at least 15 per cent and by setting up industries to produce substitutes for imports. This in turn led to the belief, encouraged partly by the success of the Marshall Plan in the reconstruction of Europe, that with a few billion dollars of aid and some technical assistance the developing countries would 'take off' into self-sustaining growth in ten to fifteen years. By the late 1950s, when these prospects had begun to look somewhat unreal, development economists and social scientists began to look for other factors and prerequisites. The earliest of these to be taken up was education; but the spread of education, it was soon discovered, without a corresponding change in attitudes to manual work or without opportunities for rural development, could only turn out a large number of white-collar workers who would neither be willing to stay in the villages nor be able to find enough jobs in the city. In the 1960s, the debate had shifted to attitudes and incentives. Later it moved to the role of economic policies and institutions. Since the early 1970s, agriculture and the small farmers have headed the list of possible approaches in the search for more meaningful development alternatives.

One of the earliest lessons of development economics presented to most developing countries was the need to increase the rate of savings and investment at least partly by transferring surplus labour from the traditional to the modern sector. The key assumption in this approach was that the traditional, mainly agricultural sector, would not respond to stimuli for change until surplus labour had been shifted to the modern sector. Then the marginal productivity of labour in the traditional sector would begin to improve, with more machinery and capital provided by the modern sector in the second phase. The social implications of creating a modern sector by squeezing a surplus from the traditional sector were hardly considered.

Even in countries which somehow managed to push up their rates of investment and growth by squeezing savings from the traditional sector or by larger access to external assistance, the problems of income distribution and of employment became more serious. As a result there is now much greater concern in development literature with problems of poverty, policies of employment and income distribution and the plight of the 'poorest 40 per cent' in developing countries. But it is seldom realised that marginal changes in income distribution will not automatically lead to a basic structural change.

During all these years there were no doubt some development economists and isolated thinkers who presented a wider and more realistic view of development problems, but the cumulative understanding of the majority of development economists in the West, and in most of the developing countries themselves, has lagged behind the reality and complexity of development problems. Only in the last four or five years has there been widespread recognition of the basic inadequacy of development models so far presented to developing countries. The search for more meaningful and viable development alternatives has now begun but, in the process, these countries have literally lost more than two decades of precious time, have added at least 50 to 60 per cent to their impoverished populations and are now confronted with more serious domestic problems because the limited economic progress they have achieved has further aggravated the inequalities of incomes within the society.

Even after the inadequacy of the past thinking on development and of the development models followed so far has been recognised, there seems to be considerable reluctance to face squarely the political and the social dimensions of development. Political factors are essentially considered as constraints on the feasibility of various alternatives; social objectives are converted into formulae of income distribution or employment opportunities, rather than pursued in a broad and positive context. There is as yet no consensus, intellectually or conceptually, on all the objectives of development. It is perhaps commonly accepted now that the first objective of development should be to meet everyone's basic needs (food, clothing, shelter, education, health, sanitation, clean drinking water and some public transport) but beyond that the consensus breaks down. Is freedom more important, or equality? Is self-reliance a better policy or greater inter-dependence? Are cultural growth and social harmony more important for man's survival, or technological progress? A careful study of the Chinese experience can provide new insights in the continuing search for answers to these questions.

LESSONS OF THE CHINESE EXPERIENCE

China's development objectives are deeply embedded in its overall political and social philosophy. The Chinese want to build a modern progressive economy, they want to achieve sustained growth in industrial and agricultural production and, above all, they want full employment and an equitable distribution of the country's resources and incomes. But in China these development objectives are subservient to the broader, political goal of building a socialist society. A great deal has already been written on China's interpretation of socialism and on its success in building a society based on socialist ideology. It is important, however, to distill from this analysis the main elements of China's development and economic policy and then examine how China's political and social philosophy has shaped or guided each of these elements.

In the early 1950s, China's economic policy was largely based on the Soviet model of emphasising heavy industry and urbanisation financed by a surplus squeezed from the rural sector and supported by strict political control by the party from the top. But the Chinese leaders realised fairly soon that the pattern of rapid industrial growth, at the cost of agriculture, was hardly suitable for a country where 80 per cent of the population lived in rural areas. Even in political terms, a rigid central hierarchy was inappropriate to the Chinese tradition, which needed a decentralised system of local leadership which could mobilise and motivate the rural population as it had done during the liberation struggle.

By 1956–7, China began to evolve its own approach to socialism, based on agricultural and rural development. Initial efforts relied on traditional factors, namely labour, intensive water control and management and organic manures since, in this phase, the social transformation of agriculture was the primary objective. But from the early 1960s a start was made on the technical transformation of agriculture. After substantial progress in agriculture and industry between 1960 and 1975, a third phase of rapid mechanisation in agriculture and selective modernisation in industry has started. The transition from one stage to the other and the timing and objectives of each phase were not smooth and easy. For example, the process of social transformation and collectivisation of land went too far in 1958, but in 1961 the size of the commune was reduced to a more realistic level and the production team was re-established as an accounting unit, while allowing for selective collectivisation of other activities at successive levels. Similarly, initial efforts to achieve rural industrialisation were unrelated to local needs, to considerations of technology and to economies of scale and had to give place to a more gradual approach, based on local needs and resources with more systematic linkages to industrial activities at the county or provincial levels.

The most striking aspect of the Chinese experience in the context of a labour surplus economy, referred to earlier, is their success in generating a surplus in the traditional rural sector and in keeping it there to modernise the traditional sector itself and in gradually creating a modern sector but generating resources for this purpose from within that sector through the rapid development of skills and the careful adaptation of technology.

As explained in Chapter 4, the rural surplus was initially generated by mobilising the underutilised labour for improved land and water management and subsequently by gradual improvements in agricultural technology. The surplus was retained in rural areas through the taxation system, which levied a fixed amount of tax expressed in monetary terms. With increasing agricultural production, total agricultural taxes as a proportion of total agricultural output have declined from about

12 per cent in the 1950s to less than 5 per cent in the 1970s. The agricultural pricing system, under which a higher price is paid for grains contributed by communes over and above their basic grain quota, and the co-operative marketing arrangements for agricultural products to the exclusion of middlemen, which in most other developing countries generally take away more than their due share, also helped to retain the surplus in rural areas for the benefit of the rural population. At the same time, in mobilising its surplus labour force the Chinese did not follow the alternative of shifting people from the traditional and familiar surroundings of village life to an impersonal and often inhuman environment of city life in which they obtain the means of survival but only become mere cogs in a vast economic machine. The Chinese created opportunities for work and for a better life within the rural areas and provided a whole new perspective on the urban – rural division of labour and the concept of primary accumulation.

Another important lesson of the Chinese experience is their ability to adopt and implement the concept of basic needs as the main pillar of their development policy long before it became a fashionable part of development literature in the West. China extended its five guarantees as early as the mid-1950s and evolved a system of ownership, production and distribution which would make these guarantees effective.

In the inherent conflict between equality and freedom, which is perhaps the most serious dilemma facing man at present, China opted for equality because, without this option, the objective of meeting everyone's basic needs could not have been fulfilled. The concept of basic needs implies a *social minimum* for the under-privileged, but there is a corresponding concept of *social maximum* which curbs an individual's freedom to increase consumption beyond the prescribed limits. This is enforced by the production pattern which does not supply luxury goods, by an ownership pattern which does not give larger incomes to anyone, and by an ideological movement which frowns on wasteful consumption. There are also restrictions on the movement of people. The average Chinese does not have full freedom to choose a new place of residence or a new occupation since the society's needs for his services are considered more important than his own assessment of his capacities or his preferences. This policy was also necessary in order to retain the rural population in the countryside and avoid the problems of urban unemployment and was accompanied by a policy of improving conditions of life in the rural areas. But these constraints or limits on freedom of consumption, occupation or mobility do not imply total denial of individual freedom in China. The freedom of expression, through posters and within groups and communities, is surprisingly high, and within a given economic unit or organisation the individual has now increasing possibilities of horizontal or vertical movement.

There is thus no segment in China which can be called privileged but there is no one whose basic needs are not met. There are regioñal inequalities, but there is no unemployment and the degree of inequality in incomes and in economic opportunity is narrower than almost all other countries in the world. China has thus succeeded in creating an egalitarian society and evolved a pattern of development which has achieved technological progress without destroying the environment or creating an energy shortage. It has utilised all its surplus manpower without uncontrolled urbanisation. This does not mean that these achievements have not involved costs and difficulties but, contrary to popular misconception, China has not sacrificed the individual. In fact, as already explained in the preceding chapter, the country has evolved a judicious blend of material and non-material incentives, and the focus of the whole system is man, his motivation and his well-being, but only after the society as a whole has been re-organised in a manner that suppresses or minimises exploitation of one group by another. But the individual must satisfy his needs only as a part of the community. If there is conflict between his welfare and collective good the latter must prevail.

In evolving its own model of socialism, China has not only presented explicitly or implicitly its own interpretation of certain basic economic concepts but provided some remarkable new lessons in relating economic factors to social and political factors.

From the very outset, Chairman Mao's writings have concentrated on the relationship between political, social and economic forces, and emphasised that the welfare of the masses can be ensured only if the masses have effective political power. For the same reasons, economic and technical progress, unless it is subservient to the political philosophy of socialist ethics and welfare of the masses, will be counter productive, because it could lead to selfishness and exploitation of the poorer and less-privileged segments of the population. In Article 22 of *Sixty Work Methods*, circulated in February 1958 and referred to in Chapter 3 (page 24), Chairman Mao dealt with this subject in the following words:

> The relationship between redness and expertness, politics and work is the unity of two opposites. The tendency to pay no attention to politics certainly must be. criticized and repudiated. It is necessary to oppose the armchair politicians on the one hand and the pragmatists who have gone astray on the other.
>
> There is no doubt whatsoever about the unity of politics and economics, the unity of politics and technology. This is so every year and will forever be so. This is red and expert. There will still be the term of politics in the future, but the content is changed. Those who pay no attention to ideology and politics and are busy with their work all day long will become economists and technicians who have gone astray and are dangerous. Ideological work and political work guarantee the accomplishment of economic work and technical work, and they serve the economic foundation. Ideology and politics are also the supreme commander and the soul. As long as we are a bit slack with ideological work and political work, economic work and technical work will surely go astray.

Some new material has recently become available which provides fresh insights into China's development strategy and into the processes by which solutions are being found for the inevitable conflicts and contradications. The most important of these are a previously unpublished collection[1] of speeches and writings of Mao Tse-tung, covering the period 1955–68, and the documents of the Fourth National Congress held in January 1975. The first set of documents brings out very forcefully Mao's constant preoccupation with charting and consolidating the course of China's socialist transition. How can the extent of collective ownership in the countryside be raised until the contradictions between agriculture and State-owned industry and between urban and rural sectors have been overcome? What portion of rural production must be saved and reinvested before allowing consumption to rise? How can industry be run on more democratic and innovative lines?

These documents, read in conjunction with some other writings on different principles of China's economy, offer some interesting explanation of the Chinese approach to certain basic concepts in economics and sociology. Some of these are discussed below.

The law of value and prices. According to Mao, the laws of value and prices have a definite role under socialism but this should not be at the expense of planning. The hard core of the Chinese economic system is still based on the socialist concept of value, which determines the value in exchange (i.e. the price) of goods in terms of the labour input. This is reflected, for example, in the relatively low price at which grain is issued to a member of the commune and given to the State against the basic quota. But this basic system is supplemented by selective use of the price system for certain definite objectives. For example, a commune which can produce in excess of its quota and internal needs can sell the surplus to the State at a price 40 per cent higher. Similarly, certain goods like bicycles and radios are sold at a price higher than their cost of production, as measured in terms of labour input, to keep their consumption down and to collect some revenue for the Government.

The purpose of planning. The main objective of the planning process in China is not to produce a 'balanced' economy but to mediate between the imbalances which provide the motive force for further development. Planning should not be at the expense of local initiative and self-reliant development. Mao's reference to 'imbalances' in this context is different from that suggested by Hirschman.[2] The basic objective of planning in China is to improve the capacity of a large number of decentralised planning entities (from production team to province) and to identify their needs, mobilise their own financial and human resources to meet these needs and distribute the benefits created on the basis of socialist principles. In the process, there will be an excess of certain goods which cannot be absorbed 'locally' (within the given planning entity) and there will be unfulfilled requirements for certain goods which cannot be produced 'locally'. The planning system at the successive level should take care of such imbalances within certain broad objectives, targets and policies laid down at the national level which will also influence the initial pattern and direction of planning at each level.

Pattern of ownership. According to Mao, ownership is not everything. How distribution is handled and how individual producers relate to one another within the collective or State-owned unit are equally important factors in the socialist relations of production. The management has to decide, for example, how much to reinvest and how much to 'distribute' to workers or members through higher wages. The pricing policy for different products also affects the actual 'surplus' value of an enterprise. These problems, which arise both in industry and agriculture, have not been fully resolved in China but the task has been facilitated by a sustained improvement in the productivity of labour without a corresponding increase in capital (in the neo-classical sense) which is one of the most important lessons of China's development experience.

Basic relationships in society. Another continuing and related theme of the present Chinese approach concerns basic re-lationships within a society. These should not be determined only by methods of production (feudal or capitalistic) but by social and political forces that will end exploitation. 'Though the relations of production should not go too far beyond what the existing level of productive forces justified,' Mao emphasises, 'they should lead the way and certainly never lag behind.'

Continuing contradictions. According to Mao, 'the socialist tradition cannot mark time too long without running the risk of retrogression. The contradiction between the collective sector (mainly agriculture) and the State-owned sector (mainly in-dustry) is the most dangerous and the weakest point during the transition.' China has not followed the usual socialist policy of pre-empting the maximum possible 'surplus value' for the State, through terms of trade, heavy taxation or maximum State-ownership of means of production. Land is collectively owned in China, and not by the State, and the level of taxation is low (3 to 5 per cent) and fixed in absolute and not relative terms. The rural sector can largely retain its surplus for further investment or distribution to improve consumption. But in industry the State sector is very large. As the interaction between collective agriculture and State industry (through agricultural machinery and chemical fertilizer) increases these problems will become more serious, but it seems that China, unlike the Soviet Union, will continue to use industrial expansion to support the agricultural sector and will not transfer resources from the rural sector to the State or the urban sector.

If China's development strategy and its underlying principles as they have evolved since 1950 are compared to the evolution of what might be called Western thinking on development, which in turn influenced development strategies of many developing countries, it will be clear that, at least so far, the world has learnt very little from China.

Even if there are some differences in the quantitative assessment of China's progress and there are questions about the costs and constraints of the Chinese system, the Chinese development model and, in particular, its approach to rural development has already demonstrated some important principles, criteria and guidelines which, taken together, constitute a valuable framework which those who wish to understand, promote or evaluate rural development must study very carefully.

A STRATEGY OF RURAL DEVELOPMENT

An attempt is made in the remaining part of this chapter to spell out the main elements of a strategy of rural development based on the Chinese approach. It starts with a discussion of the basic objectives of rural development, the constraints on or linkages between various objectives and some of the main policy implications. It then identifies certain key elements of the model on which its replicability largely depends. These in turn lead to a set of economic, social and political criteria for the efficacy of a particular rural development strategy or for the evaluation of its results.

While this strategy and its various elements are based on the Chinese experience, their validity as a conceptual framework will not be affected by the assertion that China's actual practice or policy on a particular point is different or that China has not yet achieved all the objectives in every respect.

The basic objective of rural development derived from the Chinese experience may be summarised as follows:

To organize, develop and utilize the available resources of land, water and manpower in such a manner that the entire rural population dependent on these resources has an equal (or at least an equitable) opportunity to meet, as a minimum, their basic needs of food, clothing and shelter with reasonable facilities for education and health and can live together in a positive and healthy social environment.

This basic objective which should be seriously considered by other developing countries has a significant *economic* component, because the basic needs of the entire rural population cannot be met without a sustained increase in agricultural production and that, in turn, requires investment, inputs, technology and trained manpower. It also has an important *social* component because the objective of equal or equitable opportunity to develop and share the available resources cannot be achieved unless the initial and subsequent distribution of income and assets is equitable and there are adequate employment opportunities for everyone. The *political* component of this objective must include a distinct improvement of the economic and social relationship to create a positive and healthy social environment. It must also include a capacity to ensure the effective and harmonious attainment of all the other objectives, through political leadership with mass participation at local and higher levels.

KEY ELEMENTS OF THE MODEL

As already mentioned, the Chinese political system and its ideological motivation based on non-material factors and rooted in its traditions of discipline and hard work are all an important part of China's development policy and experience. But to understand the Chinese model of development, it is necessary to identify certain key elements or end results of the model and then explore if these can be sought under any other political system or ideological framework. In technical language this would mean that China's peculiar political or historical background might be treated as exogenous factors, and distinguished from certain endogenous factors in order to determine the consistency and replicability of the model. In practice this would in no way minimise the importance of political factors, but would only provide greater flexibility in choosing a wider range of political options or prerequisites to seek the desired end results or 'elements' of the model.

The starting point for the proposed model of rural development, based on the Chinese approach, is provided by the objectives of rural development suggested above, which must be pursued simultaneously. If a certain model can achieve rapid growth of agricultural production, but adversely affects the distribution objectives or leaves out the basic needs of the poorest quarter of the population, then it would not meet the minimum criteria. The model, which is presented without prejudging its feasibility in different situations, would also be of little relevance to countries in which rural development is pursued in pure economic terms to the exclusion of social and political objectives.

The *first* and perhaps the most important element of the model is an equitable distribution of land and other rural resources. If these resources are unevenly distributed and the top 5 or 10 per cent of the rural population owns and controls a large proportion, say one-third to one-half of the total land, and the bottom 30–40 per cent of the rural population has only 5–10 per cent of the land, very few objectives of rural development can be achieved. The underutilised labour that is potentially available in the rural areas will not be fully utilised, the distribution of rural incomes could become even more inequitable and the basic needs of the poorest segment of the rural population will be difficult to meet because they cannot really benefit from any irrigation or other technical improvement that may be achieved. Drastic land reforms in favour of the poorest segments of the rural population are thus the first essential prerequisite of rural development.

The *second* important element is the organisation of the rural population for collective or co-operative activities appropriate to the stage of development and to the level of technology that has been reached. This would include ability to mobilise the unemployed and underemployed labour force for improving the land, undertaking irrigation and water-control projects or building rural roads and, in subsequent stages, ability to divert manpower for other activities and improve agricultural technology. It would also require the gradual evolution of an institutional framework that would lead to sustained technological improvements and a steady increase in modern inputs such as fertilizers, pesticides, better seeds and machinery when needed.

Land reforms reduce inequality but by themselves can seldom lead to a sustained increase in agricultural production without some degree of collectivisation. In countries where land is scarce and labour is surplus, the average size of holdings seldom exceeds 1 hectare. Small farmers with such a small patch of land cannot sink a tube-well, acquire a pump or use agricultural machinery; often they cannot acquire the knowledge or the financial means to adopt new technology. In essence, the case for collectivisation[3] rests on four important factors: (i) the need to mobilise surplus labour force for land and water development, which requires a sizeable land area; (ii) pooling of savings and investable resources; (iii) uniform sharing of knowledge and technology; (iv) greater specialisation and better management. But a more important justification is a distinct improvement in social relationships and a much more equitable distribution of incomes when land is collectively owned by those who cultivate it.

There are, of course, many ways of collectivising land or related economic activities: State farms owned by the Government in which the farms are run by qualified experts and the workers are wage-earners; a pattern of service co-operatives in which land is privately owned by an individual or a family but one or more co-operatives provide most of the inputs needed and market the produce on behalf of the owners; and communally-owned farms or producers' co-operatives. Each of these patterns can be supplemented by co-operatively-owned industries and special projects or programmes which can pool the surplus labour force in slack periods for labour-intensive works.

In the case of State farms, certain aspects such as mechanisation, cropping pattern and technological improvements can be handled more efficiently, but the people working on the farms are essentially wage-earners who do not take part in decision-making or have a sense of participation in rural development. Similarly, in the case of service co-operatives superimposed on private ownership, relatively large owners tend to pre-empt the bulk of the services, and the pattern of social relationship in the rural community can seldom be preserved. It is also more difficult to avoid the multiplicity of different kinds of co-operatives with overlapping loyalties and functions. Considering all these factors, the best form of collectivisation is achieved, at least initially and perhaps for a considerable period of time, through units which are communally owned by all their members who develop their own arrangements for decision-making on such matters as cropping patterns, organisation of work and distribution of benefits within the broad policy guidelines coming from above. There are, however, serious cultural or sociological obstacles which affect the creation and operation of producers' co-operatives. In practice, each county has to choose its own pattern of collectivisation or communal ownership in the light of its.own peculiar political and cultural circumstances.

It is important to emphasise that the concept of collectivisation does not imply a continuous and indiscriminate enlargement of the size of the collective. It must be related not only to the cultural or ethnic situation but also to the optimum scale for a particular activity and to the efficiency of the labour force resulting from greater specialisation. In China, for example, the actual unit of cultivation and of accounting is relatively small – the production team of twenty to thirty families, or sixty to ninety workers, which corresponds to a natural village – but certain other activities are collectivised at the brigade level and others, including the administrative and political functions, at the commune level, which also corresponds to the traditional market area. In this way basic rewards are related to work in the production team, but these are supplemented by income from other collective activities undertaken by the brigade and the commune. At the same time, each member has a sense of participation in the development of the rural economy which is important for the attainment of the social objectives of rural development.

The *third* key element is the capacity of the rural population for diversifying its activities to ensure increasing social productivity in a growing population, more employment opportunities and rising incomes. An expanding labour force in rural areas cannot be absorbed indefinitely solely in labour-intensive cultivation or irrigation projects; there must be a gradual diversification of the rural economy into fisheries, forestry and animal husbandry and especially into rural industries. These activities and related services such as distribution and transport will generate more employment and also create additional incomes for the rural population which in land-scarce countries cannot meet their basic needs only from the cultivation of land. Diversified activities also provide a greater sense of participation and fulfilment for the rural population. There will be constraints of resources, skills and markets before such diversification can be successful, but their removal will depend partly on the size of the unit undertaking the programme and partly on the degree of success achieved in increasing agricultural productivity in the initial phases. As already pointed out, in China a growing proportion of rural incomes is now being obtained from non-agricultural activities that are collectively owned and managed.

The *fourth* important element in this framework is the gradual but active promotion of a policy of social development. This has three interrelated components: the expansion of education and health facilities and other social services to the extent possible through the community's own financial and human resources; efforts to improve employment and income distribution; and greater harmony in social relationships. The expansion of education and health facilities is critically important in the development of human resources and so is the nature of social relationship. In the final analysis, the objective of social development goes beyond the narrow concept of social justice and better income distribution. Oppression and exploitation by the land-owner, the local official or the middle-man are an essential ingredient of poverty in many countries and these must be eliminated through land reforms, administrative reforms or other institutional devices which not only impose ceilings on larger holdings but also change the social and political relationships in the rural areas. But after these negative barriers to social progress have been eliminated, there is need to create a positive social structure which will give dignity, self-respect and a sense of participation to every member of the society and which will enable them to live and work together in a healthy and dynamic social environment.

And *finally*, any viable framework for rural development must provide for political and administrative capacity to link the particular rural community with the rest of the economy and to resolve the conflicts which will inevitably arise between different interest groups within the community and often with outside interests. In China, the communes evolved initially as fairly self-contained marketing units but gradually various communes began to exchange or pool products, agricultural inputs and often labour for bigger projects. As explained in Chapter 5 (page 79), the scope of these inter-commune relations are now expanding further with the county as the focal point for rural industrialisation. The administrative arrangements by which a 'unit' of rural development is integrated with the rest of the economy will have to be based on many important considerations, namely the size of the unit and its capacity to meet its needs and the nature of its relationship with other areas and with the needs of the urban population. Farmers should produce more because they can eat more and not only to provide cheap food to urban areas. The administrative and political framework for rural development must be evolved first on a just theory of distribution which protects the legitimate interests of the rural population and, second, on the most appropriate and horizontal division of labour which is closely related to the economic and technological progress of the population. No rural community can achieve sustained progress if it is directly or indirectly exploited either by the tax system or the terms of trade under which it operates.

The ultimate success of the proposed strategy of rural development will, however, depend largely on the strength of the political system to generate a minimum of non-material motivation supplementing the limited material rewards which a developing economy with limited resources may be able to promise. Each country must discover its own objectives or ideological premises which will involve and motivate the population, but some common and often mutually reinforcing factors might be greater emphasis on shared austerity, the principle of rural co-operation and greater equality in the distribution of benefits. The commitment of top political leadership to these objectives must be accompanied by effective political mechanisms at the local level. Otherwise the strategy will begin to crumble at different stages of implementation.

These key elements of rural development strategy are interrelated and one of them may be more critical than the other in different situations. Again, in a carefully devised strategy they can reinforce each other. The practical implications of these elements for other developing countries are discussed further in Chapter 7.

CRITERIA

Different developing countries have formulated their agricultural and rural development objectives differently but very often the main emphasis is on economic and technical aspects of agricultural development. The social and political objectives, if any, amount to no more than pious hopes or familiar rhetoric. The social and political objectives, even when they are spelled out concretely, are seldom backed by concrete policies and political direction. The actual conflicts and inconsistencies between various objectives are not clearly identified. The agricultural targets, for example, are generally worked out in great detail, with specific targets for different crops based on demand and export projections, supported by elaborate calculations of the possible increments from additional area and increased productivity, and specific programmes for irrigation, fertilizers and research. But apart from public investment, which is generally expensive in terms of expected economic benefits, and some policy measures to provide subsidies or support prices, there is seldom any assurance that these centrally determined production targets can really be achieved. The most important source of potential capital and of increased productivity is the surplus manpower available in the rural areas. But the utilisation of this surplus is intimately linked to the pattern of land-ownership. If one-fifth or one-quarter of the rural population are landless they can hardly benefit from an irrigation project or fertilizer subsidy. Similarly, the income distribution objectives are seldom an integral part of the overall development strategy. In some countries redistribution of income has been achieved through specific policies and programmes providing, for example, more credit for small farmers, special services for the rural poor, education, training and special development schemes for backward areas. But these do not tackle the basic causes of inequality or poverty which are partly related to ownership of land and partly to social relationships. The creation of rural employment can only solve a part of the problem by preventing the poorest segments of the rural population from starving. The fulfilment of the basic needs of the poorest segments of the population and provision of a socially positive and healthy environment will not be attained until this segment has more equitable access to land and other rural assets.

If there is agreement with the basic premise of the theoretical framework presented in this chapter, that the main objective of a development strategy is to eliminate or at least reduce poverty and to meet everyone's basic needs, then it will be possible to devise a criteria for determining the consistency and inter-relationship of different elements of a particular rural development strategy or for judging its results.

The *economic* elements of the criteria would include the utilisation of available manpower in the rural areas; means of improving agricultural technology and uniform access to improve technology for all the farmers in a given unit or region; availability of agricultural inputs; and the capacity of the rural community to achieve a sustained increase in rural incomes and rural consumption through larger agricultural production and diversified activities such as fisheries, forestry, animal husbandry and especially rural industries.

The *social* criteria, similarly, should seek a continuing increase in employment opportunities to absorb not only the pool of unemployed and underutilised workers but also future additions to the rural labour force, improvements in income distribution in rural areas, the provision and improvement of health, education and other necessary social services, and a gradual process of social development in which each member can begin to have a sense of participation, dignity and self-respect as a part of a dynamic social organism.

The *political and administrative* criteria must evaluate the capacity of the system to provide leadership and guidance from above without curbing local participation and initiative, the creation of organisational and institutional links which will relate and integrate the rural economy with the national and provincial goals, targets, policies and programmes, and the impact of the overall planning apparatus and economic policies on agricultural and rural development objectives and policies.

The vigour with which these and other relevant criteria can be developed and applied would partly depend on the concreteness of the underlying objectives but also on the degree of decentralisation achieved in the processes of planning and implementation.

The following chapter examines the key question of the relevance of this model to other developing countries and identifies some essential prerequisites for each of the main elements of the model. The implications of partial or intermediate solutions are discussed in Chapter 8. A brief evaluation of some other experiments in rural development in the light of the criteria suggested above is presented in Appendix C.

7

Relevance of the Chinese Experience for Other Developing Countries

When the Chinese themselves are asked if other developing countries could adopt their system or model of development they invariably say that every developing country must find its own solution to its problems in the light of its political, social and economic circumstances.

There is a great deal of proverbial Chinese wisdom in this answer, since there is hardly a country which could blindly replicate or reproduce the Chinese model of development in all its manifestations. Even in countries whose objectives and political circumstances are similar, the Chinese model would have to be carefully tailored and adapted to the peculiar requirements of that country.

In many ways China is unique. First of all, it is a very large country, in fact the largest in the world in terms of population, with an unusual capacity for geographical isolation and with a large domestic market. The vagaries of international politics in the post-war era also forced China into political and economic isolation for almost two decades and further strengthened its resolve to build a self-reliant inward-looking economy. China's capacity for collective effort has its roots in its tradition of discipline and hard work and in its prolonged struggle to control its large and untamed rivers. Finally, its political system has evolved under the guidance of great and dedicated leaders such as Mao Tse-tung and Chou En-lai who had the unprecedented opportunity of leading their people for more than half a century.

Partly because of these peculiar features and partly because of the relative paucity of more detailed information, most scholars and writers on China, including many whose visit to the country left them very impressed with its achievements, have been treating China as a world apart. They assume, explicitly or implicitly, that China's model cannot be easily replicated in other developing countries. Some 'lessons' have, of course, been emphasised from time to time, such as using more labour and less capital, the need for simpler and more appropriate technology, the example of barefoot doctors and the participation of the people in development. But to my knowledge, the relevance of China's overall experience for other developing countries has not yet been faced squarely in the current debate on development alternatives.

Even if we consider China's size and its political background as unique features, we cannot ignore certain common elements which China shares with other developing countries. China started its struggle for development about the same time as most other developing countries of Asia and Africa. Its backlog of poverty was, in fact, larger than in most other countries and, like many other developing countries, China had limited cultivable land (98 million hectares for a population of 500 million) with 80 per cent of its people living in rural areas. And yet in these twenty-six years it has eliminated absolute poverty, succeeded in providing gainful employment and a basic minimum living standard for its massive population along with a relatively equal distribution of incomes. Beyond that, China has evolved a social and economic structure which has given a sense of dignity and participation to the average Chinese while preparing for rapid technological and economic progress in the future.

Of the 2000 million people living in the developing world (excluding China), 1500 million live in rural areas and at least half of them suffer from absolute poverty and chronic hunger. Despite more than two decades of impressive economic progress in the world as a whole and in many of the developing countries themselves, the actual size of this unfortunate segment of humanity has been increasing. What is the solution to their problems, particularly in those developing countries where the availability of land per capita is less than 1 hectare and where the industrial or urban sector, even with optimistic assumptions on future investment and production, is absorbing only a small portion of the increase in the labour force? In answering this question, these countries simply cannot ignore the lessons of the Chinese experience.

It is seldom possible to describe or understand a socio-economic system without some moral judgements which inevitably arise from certain ethical beliefs or pre-conceptions. The long-term viability of a society, in fact, depends on its ability to evolve a consensus or at least a common 'feeling' about the proper way of conducting its affairs. In practice, all economic systems are based on certain institutions, practices and ideals which, taken together, constitute its ideological and ethical foundations and its political philosophy. In some societies, the political philosophy is explicit and therefore illustrated by theories, strategies and programmes; in others, the political philosophy is implicit and often difficult to define, with many views which clash with each other and often change over time. It is obvious that no ideological or metaphysical solution can provide satisfactory answers to all the problems for an indefinite period, but it is also true that certain concepts or ideologies do tend to sweep the world at certain periods of its history.

The people of Africa, Asia and Latin America are today confronted with certain fundamental choices for re-ordering and restructuring their societies. These are presented to them under various labels – capitalism, democracy, liberalism, socialism, communism and Marxism – and various mixtures of these such as social democracy, democratic socialism and economic liberalism. Each of these labels has acquired certain geopolitical connotations which appear 'good' or 'bad', 'desirable' or 'undesirable', depending on the geographical and political situation of the country concerned.

In understanding or analysing the Chinese approach and in determining its relevance to other developing countries, one must not be mystified by these labels. In the post-war debate on different systems, and particularly in the context of cold-war politics, certain intellectual barriers have arisen which are difficult to overcome if one's vision is confined to a particular system and its analytical tools or policy manifestations. The problems of developing countries today are very different from those of Western Europe and America in the nineteenth century and of Eastern Europe in the beginning of the twentieth century. In making their choice they must disentangle the alternatives from all the prejudices which have arisen either from cold-war politics or from the intellectual barriers dividing different viewpoints.

The developing countries have before them many important lessons of history and the results of different systems but no conclusive model which they could adopt blindly without considering their own socio-economic and political conditions. The so-called capitalistic system, for example, has generated unprecedented technological and economic progress in Europe, North America and some other parts of the world for almost two centuries. This phase of capitalism has also seen the birth of ideological concepts such as egalitarianism, secularism and nationalism which in turn stimulated the gradual evolution of democratic institutions with growing emphasis on social welfare and personal freedom. These institutions also provided certain political and social parameters which not only influenced the nature of the economic and technological change but also led to a gradual change in the power structure in favour of the less-privileged classes, mainly through the trade-union movement. But the system as a whole has continued to be exploitative. The end of the colonial era has also aggravated the problems of income distribution in many of these countries. Inequalities between personal and regional incomes have increased and the whole value system has become excessively materialistic, threatening in the process some of the most precious values known to man. The scope for individual initiative has been superseded by the large corporation and the economic system is no longer 'free' either as regards movements of goods or the mobility of factors of production. The system also depends on a continuing but wasteful increase in mass consumption and involves a serious erosion of the human environment. In fact, it can be predicted that the existing patterns of production, consumption, income distribution and social relations cannot continue for very long in most capitalistic societies without drastic changes in the whole structure and a definite shift towards more egalitarian policies. Recent political trends in Western Europe represent a fascinating reaction to these problems of Western societies.

The results of socialistic experiments in different parts of the world have also been mixed. It is also widely recognised, and established by actual experience, that a socialistic system can

achieve a much more egalitarian distribution of incomes combined, at least in the initial stages, with rapid economic growth.
But the efficiency of such a system in attaining very high levels of
technological progress in subsequent stages of development has
not yet been fully established. There is also concern that the
system does not provide adequate scope for individual freedom
and initiative which is important for the realisation of his full
potential as an individual and as a member of the society. The
ideological motivation, which is supposed to replace the profit
motive or the drive for individual advancement, has also been
less than adequate in many socialist countries, necessitating
greater regimentation to force the less-motivated segment to fall
into line. Alternatively, some countries have tried to reintroduce
personal incentives on a limited scale in order to supplement the
ideological motivation with inevitable problems of achieving the
right balance or justifying the mixture.

Every country or society has, of course, the right to determine
its own development objectives and the relative priority of these
objectives. It is a moot point whether this right belongs only to
the Government in power, which may not be considered
'representative' in the real sense of the word, or to the bulk of the
population but, at this stage in history, at least for those
developing countries which have a relatively low per capita
income and widespread poverty, the elimination of absolute
poverty and satisfaction of basic needs of the entire population
should become the cornerstone of a new approach to development. If this is accepted, then the choice of strategy, policy
instruments and operational means would become easier. For the
past two decades, a majority of developing countries have
concentrated on development strategies whose primary aim was
rapid economic and technological progress, particularly in
industry and related sectors such as power and transport. There
was an underlying expectation that the additional resources
generated by economic growth could also be used to expand
social services and to expand employment opportunities for the
benefit of the poor. But, in practice, the redistribution of income
through this 'spill over' or 'trickle down' effect of economic
growth has been extremely limited.[1]

The main lesson of the Chinese experience is that, to achieve
the objective of equality of opportunity and equal distribution of

incomes, appropriate social reforms and changes must be introduced *before* the policies, programmes and institutions for economic and technological progress are initiated or set up. Otherwise, the maldistribution of the initial benefits of economic progress will make the subsequent attainment of distribution objectives increasingly more difficult. China is also one of the few socialist countries in which the ideological motivation has been successfully retained for so long, in which the concept of equality is not confined to incomes or economic relations and in which the prospects of rapid technological and economic progress are now clearly visible.

It should be clear to anyone with a sense of history that the search for development strategies geared to the basic needs of the entire society and to the objective of distributive justice combined with rapid growth, lies in the direction of 'socialism' and its basic egalitarian and collective welfare concepts. Whether a socialist pattern can be evolved with a human face and on democratic principles will depend on the degree of material and moral polarisation in the society. The key step is to persuade those who are incidental or inherent beneficiaries of past inequalities to share better with the less privileged in the future. If they refuse to accept willingly these principles of justice and morality, then harsher solutions would seem unavoidable. There is thus no single model or pattern of socialism that is readily available to all countries; every country has to evolve its own brand for its own needs and problems. Socialism in Tanzania is very different from socialism in China, which again is different from socialism in Eastern Europe.

The theoretical framework for rural development presented in Chapter 6 identified five key elements without which, it was suggested, a rural development strategy would not be viable in the long run and in most cases would not achieve all the economic and social objectives of rural development. These five elements are:

- more equitable distribution of land and other rural resources in order to give greater opportunity to the poorest segments of the rural population to meet their minimum needs;
- organisation of farming and other related activities, including land and water development, on a collective or co-operative

basis in order to ensure a fuller utilisation of available physical and human resources and more equitable distribution of future incomes;
- diversification of the rural economy within agriculture and into small and medium-scale agro-based industries to provide additional employment opportunities and incomes and to improve the pattern of rural life;
- an active policy of social development through the expansion of social services and the improvement of social relations;
- political and administrative capacity for the planning and implementation of this strategy to provide linkages with the rest of the economy and protect the legitimate interests of the rural population.

These elements reflect a mixture of goals and processes but together they constitute an integrated conceptual framework of rural development. If either of the elements is missing or becomes negative in its net impact the process of rural development will be adversely affected.

An attempt is made in the following paragraphs to identify some of the essential prerequisites or obstacles in relation to each of the five key elements of the proposed strategy and to discuss the problems of institutional transfer. As already mentioned, an essential purpose of separating these elements from the peculiar political and cultural background of China is to determine if they can be pursued under different political and cultural circumstances or through institutions or systems which may be different. China's experience, it is often mentioned, cannot be repeated in other developing countries because their political and historical circumstances are different and they lack the kind of leadership which initiated and sustained the Chinese revolution. This assertion may well be true for many developing countries but this should not minimise the need for a careful analysis of the Chinese development experience to identify in more specific terms how at least some countries might benefit from this experience.

EQUITABLE DISTRIBUTION OF LAND AND OTHER RESOURCES

A more equitable distribution of land and other resources is a highly complex political issue for developing countries. In most of them, as in pre-liberation China, the pattern of land ownership is fairly uneven, or 'skewed' as the economists prefer to call it. In India in 1970, for example, 4.46 per cent of rural households, with a population of 29 million, operated 35 per cent of the available land with holdings of 20 acres or more per household (11 per cent of land in holdings of over 50 acres); while 26.3 per cent of the rural households, or 102 million people in rural areas, had no land at all, and another 47.5 per cent of the rural households or 185 million people in rural areas had less than 5 acres (2 hectares) per household.[2] Even in a country as densely populated as Bangladesh in 1968, the top 7.8 per cent of landowners had more than 30 per cent of land while at least one-fifth of the rural population of 60 million were landless.[3] The pattern of land ownership in Latin America is even more skewed.

The first and most obvious purpose of agrarian reform is to achieve greater equality in the distribution of income by taking away land from the relatively large farmers and redistributing it to the small farmers or to the landless workers. But there are certain supplementary objectives. The pattern of land ownership often determines the pattern of distribution of credit and other agricultural inputs and, in practice, the large and medium land owners manage to pre-empt a much larger proportion of these facilities and inputs. Another aspect concerns the nature of relationships between the landowners and the tenants who cultivate the land on the basis of rent or crop-sharing and to some extent even between the big landowner and the small farmer. This relationship reflects different degrees of exploitation and dependency, depending on the local political situation, tenancy laws and customs. Apart from the redistribution of land, agrarian reforms, to be effective, must also ensure a more equitable distribution of credit and inputs and change these relationships in favour of the small farmers and landless labourers. In essence, land reforms, as clearly illustrated by the experience of China and some other countries, involve a major psychological and political transformation requiring dedicated leadership, mass participation and sometimes even violence.

The extent, nature and success of agrarian reform depends essentially on the political power structure. Perhaps the most striking feature of the Chinese Revolution was its success in transferring effective political power to the poor majority and retaining it there, without allowing some of the old poor to become the 'new elite'. Whether the developing countries of today can transfer political power to their poor majorities in the best spirit of democracy without a violent revolution depends on the degree of contradictions and antagonism that exist between different classes or segments of the society. Mao, in his famous essay *On the Correct Handling of Contradictions among the People* (op. cit.) points out very clearly that some social contradictions are antagonistic while others are not. For example, contradictions between the people and any invading enemies and those between exploiters and exploited classes are antagonistic. But contradictions among 'the people' themselves (i.e. between workers, peasants and intelligentsia) are not generally antagonistic. Even the contradiction between the exploiter and the exploited class has a non-antagonistic aspect, but antagonistic contradictions can seldom be resolved without violence.

A careful analysis of these contradictions and of the extent of antagonism which exists in a society is an important step in any programme to achieve social transformation through land reforms and other related measures. Even if all the contradictions and conflicts of interest cannot be eliminated at once, a substantial reduction in the degree of antagonism should be the primary objective of land reforms. This will involve a fairly drastic ceiling on private land-holding but accompanied by other steps which will eliminate or reduce the disability of the small farmers or tenants through appropriate tenancy laws and positive political support. This will itself bring about a gradual change in the social relationship between different segments of the rural population, reduce the dependence of the poor on the rich and increase the farmers' access to credit and other inputs.

To illustrate this important point let us take the example of a typical Punjabi farmer (in India or Pakistan) with say 50 acres of land. Although in comparative terms he will be regarded as a large landowner, he is very different from his cruel predecessor in China. He will generally be a very good innovator in agricultural technology with a good record of rising production. He will not be disgustingly rich but will be fairly well-to-do, with a capacity to re-invest a good part of his extra income in a tube-well, a tractor, fertilizer and pesticides. He probably looks after his tenants or hired workers fairly well because he needs hard and dedicated labour on his farm. But, after the first phase of development, lasting say ten to fifteen years, he will have accumulated considerable capital and will begin to expand his assets, either by buying land if there is no ceiling on land-holding or setting up small industrial units such as a flour mill or cotton-ginning factory. He will have the capacity to mechanise his farm further in order to reduce his expenditure on hired labour. He will also seek political influence or office in his area because he needs to ensure continuing access to credit and other facilities. At this stage, the contradictions between him and the people dependent on him or working for him would start becoming antagonistic. Because of his disproportionate access to land and rural incomes he would begin unintentionally to contribute to the relative poverty of a segment of the rural population in a period of rising agricultural productivity.

In a country with plenty of land and ample economic opportunities for everyone, the efforts of a typical farmer with 50 acres to improve his future would be quite legitimate and almost commendable. But, in a country where one-quarter or one-fifth of the population has no land or very little land and little hope of relieving their poverty through industrial or urban employment, a 50-acre holding with disproportionate opportunities for further progress is, to say the least, amoral. If, in such a situation, land reforms could be introduced setting certain limits on the personal aspirations of large and medium land-holders, with opportunities to use their abilities for collective welfare, the potential con-tradictions would not become antagonistic. But if the process of technological change, supported by Government investment and subsidies, enables them to acquire control of 40–50 per cent of the total land in the country, and even acquire political power to retain control, probably in combination with an industrial elite and a professional middle class, then the classical pattern of class antagonism could begin in the true Marxist sense with diminish-ing chances of a peaceful transformation of the social structure.

It is a tragic irony of the development experience of the past three decades that the distribution of income generated by economic growth has worsened and not improved the prospects of peaceful social transformation, particularly in Latin America but also in parts of Asia and to a lesser extent in Africa. But it is not too late. Political leaders in many countries genuinely want to reduce poverty and meet the basic needs of the entire population. There are obstacles arising from the presence of a large privileged class, but that class is seldom homogeneous and often includes elements which might be sympathetic to the welfare of the poor majority. There are also possibilities in some countries of a gradual change in the political power structure in favour of the poor, thus preparing the ground for more effective land reforms in the future.

But the process of social transformation is not a one-time process which will be completed with land reforms. Just as all the landlords are not bad, all the individuals that make up what are called 'the masses' are not good. It is very easy to incite them to demonstrate or to rise against the landlords, but it is not so easy to organise them into a dedicated and disciplined workforce to build up the country. That requires a positive political ideology to guide the movement. This movement may be based on nationalism, religion or any objective which will motivate and mobilise the population to work for it. In the absence of such a positive ideology and an effective political movement under strong leadership, a process of social change initiated only on the basis of agitation could rapidly lead to chaos and anarchy and the re-emergence of a new elite. It is also important to keep the gap between needs and aspirations within manageable limits, other-wise it will be difficult to keep people satisfied only by meeting their basic needs.

Even after the political prerequisites for land reforms have been met, many other problems remain. The most difficult of these is to identify a reasonable basis for redistributing the land. Should it go to the poorest and the landless or only to the small farmers in order to make them more viable or productive? Should there be a minimum size below which individual holdings should not be broken? How should other related problems like share cropping be tackled? These are extremely complex questions and more difficult to resolve in countries where the per capita availability of land is 1 hectare or less. It is also possible that a programme of land distribution will lead to an initial decline in production because the large and medium landowners are generally more efficient, and it will take some time before the new owners can acquire the means necessary to sustain and expand production. That is why the solution of these problems and, in fact, the very success of land reform will depend not only on a positive political movement to mobilise the population but also on a gradual process of collectivisation.

COLLECTIVISATION

Collectivisation of agriculture and related activities is another important prerequisite of integrated rural development. It is, in fact, impossible to devise a meaningful strategy of rural development without some collectivisation in one form or another. It will be seen from the data given in Appendix A that in fifty-five out of eighty-two developing countries the average availability of arable land for each rural inhabitant is less than 1 hectare. In only nine developing countries (six in Africa and three in Latin America) is the average availability of arable land more than 2 hectares (the maximum being 6.34 hectares in Argentina, compared to 44 hectares in Australia, 24 in Canada, 27 in the United States and 4.70 in the United Kingdom). With the population growing at 2.5–3 per cent per annum in most developing countries, and with limited prospects of labour absorption in industrial activities or urban areas, it will be almost impossible to absorb the surplus manpower and tackle the problems of small farmers and landless workers without some form of collectivisation in agriculture and related activities. In India and Pakistan, for example, the minimum size for an economically viable holding is about 3–5 hectares, in Bangladesh and Sri Lanka it is about 2 hectares, but the supply of arable land per capita is 0.55 hectares in Pakistan, 0.43 hectares in India and 0.15 and 0.13 hectares in Bangladesh and Sri Lanka respectively. In other words, even if all the land were equally distributed on the basis of this minimum viable size, that is a holding whose owners can afford a pair of bullocks and some farm implements, there will be about 20 million rural families in India, 2 million in Pakistan, 6 million in Bangladesh and about 1 million in Sri Lanka with no land whatsoever. Perhaps some of these landless could be drawn into the employment stream if the agricultural sector is making rapid progress and the labour intensity of investment policies is deliberately encouraged, but even this will not assure their longer-term future without some access to land and other rural resources. The longer-term viability of a rural development strategy must be judged in terms of its capacity to tackle the problems of the landless population and not only the small farmers.

One of the serious impediments to agricultural progress in most developing countries is the inability of small farmers to develop and utilise their water resources. A tube-well or a low-lift pump, for example, needs an average holding of about 20 hectares. A small farmer with a holding of, say, 1 or 2 hectares can perhaps sink a tube-well, if he can raise the resources, and sell the surplus water; but the location of pumps or tube-wells in relation to the distribution of surface or ground water resources and their optimum size and distribution can seldom be properly regulated if the area covered is divided into many small-holdings with each farmer having the right to participate or stay out. The engineering requirements of canals, dams and flood-protection works require even larger area coverage. If collective ownership is not possible, some other means to treat the entire land area as one engineering and economic unit must be found. The same argument applies with equal force to certain activities such as the optimum cropping pattern and plant-protection operations.

Another important justification for collectivisation, particularly in countries with surplus labour, is a fuller utilisation of available human resources. In agriculture, even if land is more equitably distributed, there are always slack periods during which the available labour force is not fully utilised. If 100, 500 or 1000 hectares are collectively owned or co-operatively farmed by, say, 500 or 1000 farmers, they can use the available manpower much more effectively. Those needed to till the available land can be given the job of tilling but others, instead of joining the stream of unemployed workers into the cities, can start levelling the land, building the embankments and improving the irrigation system. After this phase, some can start breeding fish or livestock or plant trees and, gradually, as emphasised later on in this chapter, begin to set up small industries to diversify the rural economy. In the meanwhile, those actually cultivating the land begin specialising in different operations, sharing their knowledge and experience with others; they also acquire greater experience in storing or marketing their produce. As a result, the entire holding receives a higher level of technology, the available inputs are shared equally and the available manpower is more fully utilised. By contrast, small farmers if they remain so can seldom acquire all the knowledge. and expertise in fertilizer, pesticides, seeds, irrigation, tractors and marketing.

A collective or co-operative unit has also a much greater capacity to overcome difficulties or withstand natural disasters and to pool its human and physical resources for providing the necessary services. A small farmer is always at the mercy of someone else, often a 'middle man' since Government services are generally inadequate if not inefficient, to give him credit or market his produce. The peasant in this situation generally finds himself exploited. The only way to solve the problems of small farmers is to involve and integrate them into collective or co-operative institutions in which they will improve their status. Special programmes for small farmers can seldom remove all their disabilities and a man in chains cannot be expected to walk or run.

The collective ownership or management of the means of production in which production and income is shared between all the members on an equitable basis is one of the most effective methods of ensuring an egalitarian income distribution policy. It also facilitates the problem of capital formation in the rural economy. The marginal saving rate of large farmers is invariably higher than that of small farmers because the latter have to use the extra income to meet their basic needs. In a collective system, since the distribution of income is designed to meet everyone's needs the amount saved in effect implies a cut in consumption beyond the level necessary for basic needs. And these savings are, of course, used for the benefit of all the members of the collective and not for improving the consumption of a small fraction.

But besides these economic and technological advantages, the concept of collective welfare has a strong ideological element, as discussed briefly in Chapter 5. Properly launched, as part of a broad political movement, the collective spirit can give every member a sense of participation, dignity and self-respect. It can help to curb selfishness and improves the entire structure of social relations in the society. The process of collectivisation as a part of the process of social transformation can thus create a non-material supplement to the limited material rewards which land reform or agricultural progress may bring. Any process of social change that is geared only to better distribution of material rewards can soon run into serious trouble because in a poor society, with limited land and other resources, material rewards can hardly be large enough to satisfy everyone's aspirations.

In practice, despite the overwhelming need for collectivisation to solve the problem of small farmers and rural poverty, very few countries have made much progress in this direction. This is largely because the political prerequisites for collectivisation have seldom been fully met. In some countries, land reform, which is the first step towards collectivisation, has been thwarted by the large landowners. Even among the small farmers, efforts to persuade landholders to merge their land in producers' co-operatives have been unsuccessful because in most developing countries land is the main symbol of a farmer's prestige and sense of security, and he is often unwilling to pool its ownership. Also, there are often cultural, tribal or age-old conflicts among different segments of the rural population, and it is not easy to merge them into co-operative ventures without a strong and persuasive political movement which can transcend these divisive forces.

In spite of these obstacles, collectivisation is an essential part of any meaningful strategy of rural development, and political leaders really interested in rural development must find ways and means of evolving an acceptable approach to it. The ultimate purpose of collectivisation is not only to pool land and labour but to lead to a total reorganisation of all the three segments of the rural economy, viz. the labour, input and the product markets. This reorganisation can seldom be achieved without a major restructuring of the rural institutions, and the possibility of achieving an optimum restructuring without collectivisation, particularly in a labour surplus, land-scarce economy, has not yet been demonstrated.

DIVERSIFICATION OF THE RURAL ECONOMY

Since almost all the eighty developing countries listed in Appendix A have no more than 1 or 2 hectares of land per capita and there are limited possibilities of shifting the rural population to urban areas, the basic needs of a growing rural population cannot conceivably be satisfied only through increasing agricultural productivity. Initially, agricultural production must rise for improving consumption levels and for generating savings, but before long the process of diversifying the rural economy must begin to absorb the continuing addition to the rural population and to sustain higher incomes.

The process of diversification has to be gradual and carefully planned, largely on the basis of local needs and local resources. Diversification within the agricultural sector is generally easier: fruits, vegetables, livestock, dairy, fisheries and the selected expansion of certain cash crops naturally constitute the first stage of this diversification. Diversification into industrial activities is more difficult and has to be based on a careful assessment of skills, natural resources and markets.

The first important consideration in launching a programme of diversification is the ownership of enterprises. Ideally, if land is collectively owned, the collective itself, or its higher structures, could acquire the administrative authority and financial means to set up such enterprises with communal ownership, drawing as much of the manpower as possible from within the collective structure. But even where the land is not collectively owned, these enterprises can be co-operatively owned. For example, sugar factories and rice or flour mills can be owned co-operatively or jointly by the growers and the factory workers, orchards or livestock farms by a co-operative formed out of landless workers or small farmers. These latter types of co-operatives would not prevent some inequality creeping into the pattern of income distribution, but it would be much less than in a sugar mill or a flour mill set up by a few large landowners. As a matter of principle, every rural community irrespective of the nature and degree of collectivisation should have a prior right to set up and benefit from industries to process agricultural products or provide inputs for agriculture. In addition, the system should ensure that these industries help to improve the income distribution in the rural areas by giving larger benefits to the poorest segments. In practice, an appropriate Government agency can supervise the initial establishment and management of such enterprises while workers and managers from within the rural community are being trained.

Another aspect is the linkage of these activities with similar activities in the economy as a whole. For this purpose, administrative procedures should be flexible and rural communities should have sufficient freedom to diversify their economy. But these activities have to be planned and carefully integrated with the rest of the industrial programme. A special programme of rural industrialisation, supported by resources and policy instruments, can also help to develop secondary centres of industrial activities and avoid excessive costs of locating industries in isolated locations. But the detailed planning and execution of these activities should be left to the rural communities themselves who should decide what industries and other activities they wish to set up or expand and how they propose to finance them. Central or provincial authorities should be concerned with imbalances which may arise in the integration of these local plans and in providing necessary advice and technical and financial assistance.

A programme of diversification and rural industrialisation carefully planned and implemented with local initiative and participation will provide not only additional employment opportunities and incomes to the rural population, but also much needed diversity of rural occupations and prevent surplus rural population from drifting to the main urban centres, thus further aggravating all the familiar problems of urbanisation.

SOCIAL DEVELOPMENT

As a minimum starting point, a strategy of rural development should include a rapid increase in education and health facilities in the rural areas as part of the basic needs package. But very few developing countries have the resources to provide these facilities for the entire rural population. It is even more difficult to provide them on the basis of modern standards. The only way to ensure the extension of these facilities to the bulk of the rural population is to accept the need for a new approach based on simpler and austere buildings built with local material and using, for example, paramedical personnel (on the lines of the Chinese barefoot doctors) and locally-trained teachers to supplement the fully-qualified personnel. Such an approach has been successfully tried in Sri Lanka, Loristan in Iran and Kerala in India.

The second important principle is to decentralise the responsibility for these facilities to the local communities. They must provide the land, the buildings and whatever manpower can be mobilised from within the community and also take responsibility for recurring expenditures. This kind of decentralisation is possible only if there are large rural communities organised and integrated with local administrative functions with facilities and powers to raise resources. If such viable communities do not exist, the task of any Government to provide these facilities on an adequate scale, through central or provincial budgetary resources, will be almost unmanageable and even the total costs involved will be much higher than those of locally-financed facilities.

But the process of social development, to be meaningful, must go beyond the provision of education, health and other facilities. The whole pattern of social life in rural areas in most developing countries is plagued by oppression, exploitation and frictions resulting from the activities of the landlord, the local official or the middle man. These relationships can be changed only gradually and through a political process which not only eliminates the negative aspects of social relations but also creates a positive atmosphere for healthy relations and closer cooperation. This process can be greatly facilitated by the collective spirit in which there is shared austerity and considerable reliance on non-material rewards to supplement whatever material rewards are available.

THE POLITICAL DIMENSION

The creation of appropriate political institutions at the local level to guide and implement a programme of rural development is one of the most important ingredients of a strategy of rural development. But the creation of such institutions, and their relationship with the members of a community on the one hand and with higher political echelons on the other, is an extremely complex problem.

In the first place, a viable system of rural development must provide political leadership and guidance to plan and implement various programmes and policies and to resolve any conflicts of interest which may arise, but these tasks must be accomplished without curbing local initiative and participation. The simultaneous attainment of both these objectives requires the growth of representative leadership at the local level and the delegation of responsibility to this leadership even if their initial capacity is considered inadequate.

The second problem arises from the integration of local leadership with the system of political parties and the governmental structure which the system has created. In countries with either a single-party system or a Government in which a particular political party has overwhelming mass support and governmental authority, this problem will not be as serious, since local political leadership will presumably represent the lower rungs of the political hierarchy. But in a multiparty system in which the Government in power has varying degrees of support in different parts of the country, it will be difficult to create local political institutions having harmonious relations with each other and with the Government in power. In such cases, the development of local political institutions should be closely tied to development functions and objectives, and every effort made to avoid any possible discrimination against those institutions which do not represent the party in power.

Another set of problems arises from the role of local officials and bureaucrats. The main focus of an effective rural-development strategy should be to organise the people to develop their own administrative and development capacity rather than to increase the number of bureaucrats 'to do things for the people'. But bureaucrats and technicians are needed to assist and advise local institutions. If these officials are trained to 'administer' or 'rule' the rural area it will be difficult to change their mentality and attitudes. The only way to integrate them with rural institutions as genuine servants of the people is to place them under the political authority of locally-elected leaders. Their efficiency should also be judged in terms not only of their technical or professional contribution but also of their capacity to serve and trust the people without curbing their initiative and participation.

One of the important functions of political and administrative institutions is to provide a nucleus of local planning ability and to create links with the rest of the economy. This requires that the process of planning at the national and provincial levels should be sufficiently flexible to allow scope for local initiative. A gradual process of decentralisation covering all aspects of planning and implementation, including the mobilisation and allocation of resources, would be an important prerequisite for the viability of local institutions. An important related aspect is the impact of various economic policies on rural development. If these policies are not in line with the objectives of agricultural and rural development, the efforts of local communities will not be fully successful.

Finally, the political feasibility of adopting a strategy of rural development based on the Chinese approach depends on at least two prerequisites: first, equitable distribution of rural resources and, second, a group of people who are ready to look after the interest of the masses. If these two prerequisites can be met, then the practical policies and operational alternatives for meeting all the other prerequisites and implications of the proposed strategy can be devised. If these prerequisites are not met, then a viable long-term strategy of rural development which will eliminate rural poverty and meet the basic needs of the rural population *cannot* be successfully devised or implemented.

Can these two essential political prerequisites be achieved without a major political change? Can the poverty of the poor be removed in a poor country with limited resources, without giving them an effective share in political power? Can they share political power without a violent revolution? The answers to these questions will vary from country to country, but must be found within each country according to its own circumstances and political objectives.

In the author's view there are probably about twelve to fifteen developing countries in which the political prerequisites for rural development could perhaps be met in the foreseeable future. These are countries in which the distribution of arable land is not very skewed and in which the Government in power is already committed to eliminating, or at least reducing, rural poverty. These countries could usefully adopt the main elements of the Chinese approach to rural development but in accordance with their own political and social circumstances.

There is another group of maybe fifteen or twenty countries in which the political prerequisites of rural development are only partially met. In these countries, land reforms have already been introduced, with ceilings of 20, 30 or 50 hectares on large holdings, but the distribution of land is still inequitable and one quarter to one-fifth of the rural population is landless. The relatively large landowners are no longer nakedly cruel and selfish, but the nature of relationships in the rural areas still involves a great deal of dependency and exploitation, partly arising from political, cultural or ethnic factors and partly from the poverty of the landless workers. The large and medium land-owners in these countries are no longer the main pillar of the political power structure, but the Government in power cannot alienate them. As a result they manage to pre-empt a large proportion of the credit, agricultural inputs and other facilities. In such countries, as discussed in the next chapter, certain *intermediate* solutions to problems of rural development could be explored to prepare the ground for a more comprehensive approach in the future.

In the remaining developing countries the prospects for meeting the main political prerequisites for rural development would not seem particularly bright, at least in the foreseeable future. In these countries the primary focus of development efforts is likely to remain on agricultural, as distinguished from rural, development and, if these efforts are successful, some benefits might 'trickle down' to the poorest segments of the population, although the overall maldistribution of income could continue to worsen. The scale and pace of these 'trickle-down' benefits could, however, be strengthened if the agricultural development strategy could include some special programmes or policies in favour of the small farmer. These approaches, despite such special programmes, will remain *partial* solutions, because they will seldom achieve all the objectives of rural development as defined in Chapter 6 or solve the problems of the landless workers. It is essential to save the landless workers from starvation through more jobs or mitigate their poverty through the provision of certain social services, but the real test of a meaningful strategy of rural development is its success in integrating the rural poor, including the small farmer and the landless workers, as equal members of a progressive rural community.

In discussing this admittedly arbitrary typology of countries in terms of their relative state of readiness for more meaningful experiments in rural development, some analysts may disagree with the basic assumption that countries in which the class conflict and antagonism is less severe are more ready for a gradual change in the political power structure in favour of the poor. They would perhaps argue for intensifying the class struggle to create circumstances for a violent and sudden change which alone, according to the classical Marxists, can give effective political power to the poor majority. This view has considerable logical force but its practical significance is not supported by history. In all the countries where the poor majority gained power through a violent revolution, and there are no more than a few (mainly the Soviet Union, China, Cuba), there were external circumstances which contributed to the success of the revolution. On the other hand, there are examples such as Algeria, Tanzania, Sri Lanka and Kerala in India in which the leadership has successfully redistributed incomes in favour of the poor without a violent revolution. It is therefore more realistic to hope that at least in those countries in which internal barriers to political changes in favour of the poor majority are not insurmountable, a genuine 'trade-union movement' of farmers will begin. The success of such efforts or experiments could be greatly facilitated by international support and assistance which, it must be admitted, has so far gone primarily to the rich in the developing countries. Recent initiatives to direct international assistance to the poor are welcome but they cannot succeed without some opportunity being afforded to the poor to organise themselves to benefit from such assistance.

8

The Search for Intermediate or Partial Solutions

The design of a strategy of rural development presented in Chapter 6 and elaborated in Chapter 7 is based on a comprehensive and organic view of development. The starting point for such a strategy is the objective of eliminating rural poverty and meeting everyone's basic needs in an egalitarian and positive social environment. The concept of rural poverty is essentially relative. Absolute poverty can be removed by providing certain basic goods and services but the removal of relative poverty and the feeling of discrimination or deprivation depends on many other factors, such as the gap between the living standard of the richest and poorest members of the society, the nature of social relations and the degree of exploitation inherent in the economic system. Development, if it is to eliminate both absolute and relative poverty, must be redefined as a more organic concept implying harmonious political, social and economic change.

The problems involved in launching such a comprehensive strategy of rural development based on the Chinese approach are very deep and very complex and it is important to recognise the political, institutional or technological obstacles that stand in the way.

The most obvious *political obstacles* are of course well known. If a large portion of the land is owned by a small number of landowners the well-being of the poor cannot be improved without drastic land reforms. But even in countries where the distribution of land is not uneven the problems of income distribution are not automatically solved. If a fraction of the population can acquire the means to reach modern standards of living or Western life-styles, can they be persuaded (or com-

pelled) to sacrifice these 'good things of life' and be content with
the basic needs of life until everyone else's basic needs are met?
These so-called privileged classes include not only the rich
landlords who inherited their wealth without making any effort,
but also entrepreneurs who pioneer and manage new industries
or organise exports. They also include civil servants, technocrats
or managers who work hard to contribute to national progress
one way or another. Can they be motivated to give up their
privileged position or material rewards and yet continue to work
as hard for the collective good? Can a system of checks and
balances be evolved which, while providing reasonable incentives, does not permit these privileged classes to pre-empt a
larger proportion of future incomes? Countries which have
experimented with different methods of evolving these checks
and balances, ranging from land reforms to different fiscal
devices, are already aware of the enormous political obstacles
involved. Very few countries, of course, have so far succeeded in
recreating ideological motivation on the Chinese scale, to obtain
sustained hard work for such a long period in return for limited
material rewards.

The *institutional* obstacles differ from country to country and
have to be carefully analysed in terms of the prevailing political
and social situation. Even in countries in which the availability
and distribution of cultivable land is not a serious problem, there
are serious cultural and sociological barriers in organising the
rural population to cultivate their land or improve the utilisation
of their water resources. Rural populations with their history of
tribal or ethnical feuds find it difficult to work together to set up
common co-operatives or marketing services. Dedicated civil
servants have sometimes substituted for local political leadership
and organised successful rural institutions like the Commilla
project in Bangladesh or the Anand milk co-operative in India;
but the majority of rural institutions in developing countries are
thwarted by lack of political direction from the top or inefficiency
and corruption at the local level.

Technological obstacles arise mostly from the low level of rural
education and skills with which many developing countries start,
but also from the uneven spread of technology as they begin the
process of agricultural modernisation. Very few countries can
match the Chinese farming experience spread over many

centuries or their traditional skill of building water-control works through collective efforts; but even in countries like India and Pakistan, which have successfully organised and adopted improved agricultural technology, the benefits have gone mainly to large and medium landowners. Technological obstacles are therefore partly linked to institutional obstacles since small farmers with their low level of education and inadequate financial resources cannot learn or try improved technology without the support of effective institutions to organise them. The technological prerequisites are even more important for efforts to diversify the rural economy.

ALTERNATIVE SOLUTIONS

The search for 'alternative solutions' becomes necessary because very few developing countries can readily meet all the essential prerequisites for adopting the comprehensive strategy of rural development based on the Chinese experience. But even this search for alternative solutions can greatly benefit from the perspective provided by the Chinese experience by identifying the limitations of each solution or bringing into sharper relief the real obstacles that impede further progress at different stages. It also provides a valuable set of criteria to judge the long-term impact of different solutions.

These so-called alternative solutions are numerous and have been tried, with varying results, by different countries. The range of solutions includes:

- semi-socialist models with varying political systems ranging from parliamentary democracies to military dictatorships, combined with a large measure of public ownership of industries and a network of service co-operatives for agriculture;
- high priority to agriculture, with active Government support through subsidies, extension services and price-support policies combined with land reforms, which impose ceilings on land holdings;
- special programmes for small farmers with a package of inputs, credit and other services;
- active income distribution and social-welfare policies for the

benefit of the poor but without changing the basic ownership patterns in the economy;
rural works programme to provide larger employment opportunities to the rural poor, while building local infrastructure.

Before discussing some examples of various alternative solutions it is important to draw a dividing line between those that prepare the ground for the comprehensive solution and those that merely prevent the rural poor from becoming poorer but do not improve the longer-term prospects for meeting all the objectives of rural development. The former can be called *intermediate* solutions and the latter *partial* solutions. The main distinction between these two does not lie in the nature and scale of specific programmes or policies but in their net impact on (i) the share of incomes, cumulative or incremental, that accrue to the poorest segments of the population; (ii) the nature of social relations in the society and the degree of direct or indirect exploitation; (iii) the longer-term political power structure and the share of political power enjoyed by the rural poor. A special programme to help the small farmers, for example, would constitute an intermediate solution if the ultimate share of the poorest 40 per cent in total national income goes up within say five or even ten years, but it would be a partial solution if the poorest 40 per cent, even if better off than before in absolute terms, keep receiving smaller shares of the total income.

In countries where the gap between the rich and the poor is not very large and the leadership is committed to share, even if gradually, a larger measure of political power with the poor majority, certain *intermediate* solutions can be attempted to prepare the ground for more comprehensive approaches to rural development. The main thrust of these intermediate solutions would be to organise the rural poor, including the small farmers, either in collective institutions or in more loosely co-ordinated associations or 'trade unions' of farmers to secure a large proportion of future incomes through subsidies, better prices and preferential access to credit or foreign assistance. This could, in due course, redress the balance of political power and permit more drastic land reforms and institutional changes in future. The success of this approach,[1] which essentially concentrates on the poor (i.e. the so-called periphery) without affecting, at least in the initial stages, the position of the rich (the centre), of course presumes that, as an alternative to a major social upheaval, the rich will be content to keep what they have but allow a larger share of future fruits of progress to accrue to the less privileged segments of the population. It also requires greater emphasis on simple technology, the development of human resources and austere living standards and could provide, in many countries, a more practicable transition to the end results sought by the Chinese approach – namely class equality and greater self-reliance.

In some developing countries the gap between the rich and poor is already very large and the richer classes have the political and the economic capacity not only to keep what they have but also pre-empt a larger proportion of future opportunities and benefits. The prospects for reducing rural poverty, improving income distribution or meeting the basic needs of the entire population in such countries are therefore very dim indeed. But even in these countries certain *partial* solutions, for the benefit of small farmers or the landless workers, could be undertaken. If the general pace of economic activity and the growth of the agricultural sector is rapid enough these spill-over benefits (or so-called crumbs) could be quite substantial, especially in the form of increased employment opportunities. But with growing inequalities of incomes, the nature of social relations would continue to deteriorate and prospects for longer-term social or political viability would remain precarious.

Different countries have tried different forms of rural organisation in their efforts to achieve agricultural progress or rural development. In testing the relevance or efficacy of different approaches to rural development it is important to investigate carefully the political, social and economic situation of the rural area concerned in order to identify clearly the most serious impediments to rural development. At the same time, the scope and coverage of the approach or the programme being considered should be carefully analysed in relation to the objectives that are being sought, for example with reference to the criteria suggested in Chapter 6.

The examples of different approaches to rural development discussed in Appendix C clearly show that a sustained increase in agricultural productivity can be achieved under varying conditions, but combining agricultural progress with an equitable process of income distribution for the benefit of the rural poor is a more complex issue. A viable model of rural development cannot therefore be evolved without taking into account the specific political and social circumstances of the country concerned. As the Chinese example shows, their economic and technological progress was constantly reinforced by a parallel political spiral by persuading people to collectivise, to distribute benefits equally and to accept austerity and sacrifice.

Israel is perhaps another example of rural development in which all the five elements identified in Chapter 6 have been successfully integrated. Land in the Israeli kibbutz is collectively owned, income is equally distributed and all the collectives are encouraged to diversify within agriculture and into small industries. There is no exploitation of the rural population, either through heavy taxation or adverse terms of trade, and opportunities for social services and social welfare have been constantly expanded. The rural economy is also well integrated with the rest of the economy. A key factor, like China, has been the ideological motivation of the population, but the political and cultural circumstances of Israel are obviously very different from those in China.

Another interesting example of rural development in which the five key elements of rural development can be clearly identified is *Bulgaria*. Like many other countries of East Europe, the most important factor has been close integration of agricultural and non-agricultural activities. At the same time, because of the socialist pattern of production and distribution, the benefits of agricultural progress and industrialisation have been equitably distributed. The impressive increase in per capita income (from $618 in 1960 to $1700 in 1975) is clearly reflected in the living standards of all the segments of the population and in improved social services.

Japan's example clearly demonstrates that even privately-owned small farms can be quite productive in terms of agricultural yields, provided the efforts of small farmers are actively supported by Government or co-operative institutions and by the industrial sectors. But Japan could not prevent growing disparities of incomes within rural areas and between urban and rural standards of living, despite its ability to reduce its rural population from 65 per cent in 1870 to 22 per cent in 1970.

A very interesting example of institutional changes as an essential prerequisite for rural development is *Tanzania*'s approach, discussed briefly in Appendix C. Like many other countries of Africa, Tanzania did not start with a major problem of unequal distribution of land or even a serious shortage of cultivable land. But most people lived in scattered hamlets with subsistence holdings next to their hamlets. The first step towards integrated rural development was to organise the rural population into rural settlements in which they could help themselves by providing essential social services and gradually preparing themselves for improving agriculture. The experiment started only about ten years ago and it may be premature to judge its final results, but the Tanzanian approach represents a remarkable effort to evolve a model of rural development suitable for African conditions. The most significant aspect of this model is the initiation of a gradual process of social change based on the principle of self-reliance and collective welfare before the process of industrialisation or agricultural modernisation is launched.

Another interesting case study presented in Appendix C is that of *Punjab* in India. Punjab has achieved over a twenty-year period an agricultural growth rate of 6.5 per cent; it has diversified the rural economy and has more than doubled the average rural income over this period. And yet the real incomes of the poorest 30 per cent have not seen any significant improvement, despite a substantial increase in rural wages, because of the proportion of landless population in the province.

In the remaining part of this chapter some other intermediate or partial approaches to rural development are discussed with a brief analysis of their potential and limitations.

SMALL FARMER CO-OPERATIVES

One significant intermediate approach which could eventually prepare the ground for the adoption of a comprehensive strategy is that of setting up producers' co-operatives for small farmers. In these co-operatives, which should be limited to holders of, say, 2 hectares or less, the owners might retain the ownership of land but the land must be physically pooled for purposes of cultivation. Benefits could be distributed partly in proportion to the contribution of land or other assets and partly on the basis of work done by the members of the co-operative. Since a holding of 2 hectares or less does not command all the necessary inputs and the owners are not generally in a position to undertake any sizeable projects of land improvement or irrigation, a co-operative of small farmers should be attractive to most of the owners. The incentive of farmers to join the small farmers' co-operative can be enhanced through special subsidies and substantial managerial support for the co-operatives. If credit is provided at a somewhat lower interest rate or if the rate of fertilizer subsidy is larger for co-operatives than for individual farmers, then most of the small owners would be encouraged to join.

The size of these small farmers' co-operatives and the institutional framework in which they operate would be of paramount importance. A co-operative with less than, say, 1000 hectares would not be very effective either in utilising the available manpower or in undertaking any sizeable irrigation or land-improvement project. Similarly, co-operatives with more than, say, 5000 hectares could become unmanageable, at least in the initial stages. Problems could also arise if the area covered by the co-operative is not contiguous and is interrupted by large or medium farms which are not integrated in the co-operative.

Whether membership of these small farmers' co-operatives is voluntary or compulsory would depend partly on the political support by the Government and partly on the scale of incentives since the effort of all workers is seldom uniform. But it should be possible to begin with service co-operatives to provide inputs such as fertilizer and agricultural machinery, and credit, storage and marketing facilities to small farmers and, when these co-operatives have gained the confidence of their members, they can gradually pool their land for joint cultivation. In either case, an early start should be made to create representative local institutions to manage the co-operatives, with positive political support from the top and with professional and technical advice from local officials.

The basic purpose of these small farmers' co-operatives would be to increase the productivity of the small farmers by enabling them to develop irrigation projects, install pumps or tube-wells and improve their access to inputs and technology and, at a later stage, improve their capacity to expand education and other social services. These co-operatives could also undertake, either directly or through higher 'tiers', certain diversified activities, including small-scale industries, to increase income and employment. But with adequate political support they could also increase the political and social status of small farmers in relation to large and medium farmers. If, in the meantime, appropriate land reforms can be undertaken to reduce the size of very large holdings and thus gradually diminish the political importance of large and medium land-holders, the creation of small farmers' co-operatives would in due course create the right political balance in the rural areas and prepare the ground for bigger and more viable rural institutions covering the entire area with expanded economic and administrative functions which go beyond agriculture. The manner in which this happens and the speed with which various phases of this transition can be traversed would depend largely on the degree of initial equality in the distribution of land and the political support which the Government is prepared to give to the small farmers. Financial and technical assistance from abroad, to finance the initial cost of these programmes and to permit rapid expansion of social services, could also contribute to their success.

SPECIAL PACKAGES FOR TARGET GROUPS

Another approach is to concentrate resources and attention on certain target groups such as the small farmers. A programme for the benefit of small farmers, for example, could:

(a) earmark minimum shares of credit, agricultural machinery and other inputs for small farmers and link credit worthiness to productivity rather than to ownership of assets;

(b) develop a special extension service which will combine credit, inputs and knowledge into a single package and provide it on time to all the small farmers located in a given area or locality;

(c) ensure low-cost storage and adequate marketing for the marketable surplus of small farmers, if possible through co-operative groups;

(d) organise them into groups to undertake certain programmes such as a joint irrigation or tube-well project, a
dairy project or an industrial co-operative for setting up a
sugar factory or a flour mill; and

(e) expand facilities for education, health, sanitation, for the
benefit of small farmers and the rural poor.

The strategy of rural development recently recommended by
the World Bank[2] is a good example of a special-package
approach or target-group approach. These approaches by
directing and concentrating resources on the target groups can
help to increase their productivity and incomes, but in practice
their success is dependent on institutional improvements, notably
on efforts to organise the small farmers to receive new technology
and inputs. In this respect the World Bank strategy does not go
far enough to tackle certain basic political and institutional issues
such as land reform or co-operatives. It also does not deal
adequately with the problems of 75 million landless workers who
constitute the hard core of the rural poor and in some land-scarce
Asian countries account for about 20–5 per cent of the rural
population.

The target-group approach is however a very important *first
step* in diverting credit, inputs and other services to the rural poor.
To succeed in the longer run this approach must be followed by
further efforts to organise the target groups into viable rural
organisations to take the next steps – ranging from bigger
irrigation projects to rural industries. The ultimate success of this
approach will also depend on the pattern of land ownership. If
the bottom 30 per cent of small farmers own only 5 or 10 per cent
of the land, the income-distribution effect of any irrigation or
land-development project is bound to be adverse. In such cases
specific measures will be necessary to redistribute benefits of
development projects through special subsidies or cheaper water
rates. Small farmers, along with the landless, can also be given a
growing share of new land and new rural industries and other
enterprises.

AREA-DEVELOPMENT PROJECTS

Yet another approach (reflected in Pakistan's integrated rural-development programme, Comilla in Bangladesh and Caqueta in Colombia) is to select certain geographical or administrative units with a well-defined area and a certain number of villages as a focal point for the provision of services and inputs, partly through governmental agencies and partly through local groups, and for improving rural infrastructure, particularly irrigation facilities. These development projects have the advantage of 'integrating' all the agricultural and non-agricultural aspects, including social services, but their success depends largely on the simultaneous growth of local political institutions. Such projects depend for their initial success on the efforts of the local officials and the resources available for new projects or social services. But, if the selection of these projects and the overall management is not quickly shared with the locally-elected representatives, the experiment begins to lose its political appeal. The pattern of land ownership in the area concerned is also of importance, since it largely determines the distribution of available inputs and facilities and ultimately the benefits of the programme as a whole. If the area-development approach is combined with land reform and with the formation of service or production co-operatives for the benefit of small farmers, it can provide, in due course, the higher 'tier' of certain self-managed co-operative institutions.

PRIVATE OWNERSHIP WITH STATE MANAGEMENT

Another approach is based on a combination of private owner-ship with State management. In this pattern, which is particu-larly relevant for newly reclaimed land, land is allotted to members on paper but not physically demarcated. The entire holding can thus be managed as one unit by a State organisation with qualified staff, which is responsible for all mechanical operations, aerial plant protection and distribution of seeds and fertilizer. But all the members are assigned certain plots of land which may change from time to time and on which they will undertake labour-intensive operations such as irrigation, weed-ing and harvesting. The management receives only a percentage of the gross produce while the rest is distributed among all the members.

Under this pattern the increase in agricultural productivity is substantial because of access to improved technology inputs and qualified management. It also provides for diversification because the project can undertake small and medium-scale industries, grow fruits and vegetables or other profitable crops, thus providing additional income and employment opportunities. But the project, unlike a self-governing rural community like the Chinese commune, does not ensure equal distribution of income nor create a sense of participation among members and workers. As is clear from the experience of Sudan's Gezira scheme, the members who own a share of such a productive project soon begin to employ hired workers to undertake their part of the operations and thus before long become 'mini-landlords'. Bureaucratic impediments can also arise and adversely affect potential political advantages of the project.

These disadvantages can, however, be minimised if land is collectively owned by all the members and workers and not parcelled out only to the initial members. An element of self-government can also be introduced gradually to supplement the State management in administering the project. This would provide a greater sense of participation in decision-making to all the members when their elected representatives begin to administer the project.

RURAL WORKS PROGRAMME AND THE LANDLESS

One of the most serious unresolved dilemmas in rural development is the problem of the landless poor. In most developing countries, particularly in Asia, the poorest population in rural areas are not the small farmers but the unemployed or partially-employed landless labourers.

The only fundamental solution of the landless is drastic land reforms followed by efforts to give them, along with very small farmers, a growing share of new land and new rural industries, but where these measures are not practicable, a major rural works programme could help to provide additional employment opportunities to the landless. Opportunities for building local infrastructure, and particularly for water control and management, are almost unlimited but their proper utilisation will require decentralised rural organisations to mobilise the surplus labour and determine priorities for local development.

While emphasising the importance of public-sector works

programmes for employing at least a part of landless workers in rural areas, it is important to recognise some of the limitations of this approach. The financial burden of such a programme on the budget can become excessive unless efforts are made from the outset to share a part of the outlay with the local community. A formula of matching grants will not only create incentives for mobilising local resources, through local taxation or voluntary labour, but also ensure more efficient implementation of the programme. At the same time the planning and administrative capacity of organisations responsible for the rural works programmes must be continually strengthened to enable them to undertake bigger irrigation works and certain non-agricultural activities.

Finally, the success of any longer-term rural works programme will depend on the overall progress of the agriculture sector. A successful agricultural programme with emphasis on small farmers, coupled with a rural works programme planned and implemented by locally-elected development councils or other appropriate organisations, could go a long way in improving the lot of the rural poor through higher productivity and better income distribution.

ECONOMIC POLICY AND ADMINISTRATIVE SUPPORT

Irrespective of the particular approach to rural development or form of rural organisation adopted, their success will depend on key linkages with the rest of the system, and particularly on the overall impact of economic policies and the relationship with higher provincial or national tiers of administration. If, for example, the exchange-rate policy is unfavourable to the agricultural sector, or if the fiscal policy takes away a substantial part of the additional income generated, or the industrial policy is not geared to the requirements of rural development, then the programme itself cannot go very far. The distribution of benefits from additional investments or certain policies within the rural economy will always be a problematic issue and in practice it will not be easy to identify investment opportunities or projects which will benefit the rural poor and yet lead to a rapid increase in agricultural production. The question of size or coverage is also an important practical question. A comprehensive programme of rural development may be introduced only in a few selected regions, or a sectoral approach may be adopted for rural irrigation and electrification or rural education. The relationship of these limited experiments to the rest of the rural economy, and the problems involved in extending the scope of the experiment to other regions, will have to be carefully explored.

Finally, the role of the bureaucracy versus the role of self-governing local institutions will offer a perennial dilemma in attempts to determine the ultimate political impact of the rural-development programmes. Civil servants at the local level and at the provincial and national level will continue to play a significant role in rural development. Their training and motivation should therefore continue to receive maximum attention. But exclusively bureaucratic approaches to rural development, even when devised by able and dedicated civil servants, have only limited impact because sooner or later they inhibit the growth of political institutions. In the final analysis, where the top political leadership in a country is not interested in rural development, very little progress can be expected.

9

Conclusion

The problem of rural poverty has become a central issue of our time. At least 750 million people or more than one-third of those living in Africa, Asia and Latin America are trapped in absolute poverty, and 80 per cent of them live in rural areas. They suffer from chronic malnutrition and live on the bare margin of subsistence. Two-thirds of them never go to school and very few expect to live beyond the age of fifty. They have limited access to clean drinking water or health facilities and virtually no security of employment or a decent livelihood. The unprecedented progress which the world has seen in the past three decades has simply by-passed this unfortunate segment of humanity.

Disillusioned by the model of development which most developing countries have followed so far, they are seeking more meaningful alternatives which will not only increase production but also liberate the poorest in these countries from the clutches of perpetual poverty. The nub of this search lies in alternative strategies of rural development since four-fifths of the absolute poor live in rural areas.

As repeatedly emphasised in the preceding chapters, the search for a strategy of development which will achieve equality of opportunity, eliminate rural poverty and solve the problems of employment and income distribution is not simply a matter of resource allocations, fiscal policy or distribution of foreign assistance. It involves an organic concept of development implying harmonious political, social and economic change. It concerns the entire moral and social existence of civilised man and his ability to live amicably and share equitably the material things and non-material values with other human beings. But different groups of people or nations have vastly different political, social, ethnical and economic circumstances and it would be simplistic to expect a single strategy of development to prove equally relevant or practicable in all developing countries. There is need for a spectrum of solutions which will be compatible with these varying circumstances. But at the centre of this spectrum there can and should be a comprehensive solution which is conceptually and theoretically superior and can achieve the best possible combination of development objectives. For countries in which such an ideal solution is not feasible, other second best, intermediate or partial solutions can then be evolved and tried, with a clear recognition of their limitations. It is in this context that the Chinese approach to rural development offers some key elements of a comprehensive solution.

In a relatively short period since liberation in 1949, China has:

— transformed its disorganised and impoverished village economy into viable production units capable of organising themselves to improve their land, control their water resources, apply improved technology and increase agricultural production to meet the growing basic needs of the population;
— created the nucleus of structural change and modernisation within the rural areas, giving them the capacity to diversify into industrial activities in accordance with their own needs, capacities and resources, rather than remain as the hinterland of an industrial sector built near the big cities where all surplus rural labour is forced to move;
— evolved a social system in which there is equitable distribution of income and maximum feasible social justice, while allowing adequate scope for increased consumption and economic incentives as long as these do not lead to the emergence of a 'privileged class';
— developed an administrative system in the rural areas that provides an effective link in the hierarchical chain at the lowest level while at the same time serving the role of a self-governing administrative unit for all the supervisory functions necessary at that level, including provision of education, medical and other social services. The main thrust of this administrative structure is not to 'do things' for the people but to organise and mobilise the people to do things for themselves.

These achievements, remarkable as they are, did not come about easily or smoothly. The process of social transformation of the countryside was accompanied by considerable political tension and controversy, particularly during land reforms, the socialist high-tide of collectivisation, the Great Leap Forward and the Cultural Revolution. These achievements also do not imply that China has solved all its economic and social problems. As brought out in Chapter 5 China faces many difficult problems and choices in the future but it has already succeeded in providing a minimum of *economic well-being* to the entire population, together with a *sense of security* and *sense of identity* to the average Chinese.

In the process China, it must be admitted, had to sacrifice full freedom of expression, mobility or occupation to their citizens, but at least so far these restrictions on freedom have remained within tolerable limits, mainly because of the ideological motivation generated by the system.

If this package of material and non-material needs (economic well-being, freedom, sense of identity and sense of security) is taken as a guide, no society has so far succeeded in meeting all these needs for all its citizens. The Western industrial countries, for example, have provided a very large measure of economic well-being and an unprecedented degree of individual freedom but greater freedom has also led to greater inequality. At the same time, excessive automation and a spirit of competition in all phases of life has imposed an overly materialistic and impersonal life-style and deprived many people of their sense of identity. Even the sense of security initially generated by economic improvement is now being eroded by senseless crime and growing violence. These problems of growing inequalities, over-consumption and waste require the gradual adoption of a policy of 'social maximum', not only to conserve scarce resources but to prepare the ground for life-styles that are more meaningful in social and human terms.

The ultimate utopia of human existence must be to resolve the inherent conflict between the objectives of freedom and equality and to evolve a system in which every individual's economic and political rights are protected, but does not lead to gross inequalities or the exploitation of the weak and the poor. The critical question is whether those who are incidental beneficiaries of unequal opportunities can be persuaded to share willingly with the less privileged. And if they cannot be persuaded or motivated in the name of justice and morality, are more drastic measures justified to redistribute incomes and economic opportunities? Can these measures be adopted while still preserving incentives for creative work and rewards for initiative and innovation? These questions become even more gruesome in most developing countries in which the issues at stake are not just higher wages but the ultimate survival of one-quarter or one-fifth of the population.

The manner in which China, with its widespread poverty and limited resources, has answered these questions deserves very careful study. Mao clearly perceived that economic relationships could not be changed without the realignment of social and political forces and that the basic purpose of development should be to harness and mobilise the human resources. This in turn provided a new set of development objectives based on a judicious blend of material and non-material rewards and of collective ownership and individual incentives. In this sense the Chinese concept of development is not confined to redistributing land or incomes but visualises a new social relationship based on shared austerity and greater self-reliance and requires that the process of social transformation of the rural society precede the technological improvement of agriculture.

It will be simplistic to assume that all or even most developing countries can adopt the Chinese approach to rural development in every respect but they can learn from it, in understanding the inter-relationship between political, social and economic factors in development and in determining their own longer-term objectives of development in the light of their own circumstances. In this context the search for certain intermediate or partial solutions will be inevitable but the perspective provided by the Chinese approach can help to highlight the limitations of these solutions and perhaps help to steer the longer-term course in the desired direction.

In essence, the range of alternatives which may be termed intermediate solutions implies that the main focus of development activity is geared to the needs and lives of the under-privileged. The relatively well-to-do classes are not eliminated: they keep what they have but a larger proportion of future incomes goes to the poorer segment of the population through investment programmes, policy support and social services. This process gradually narrows down the gap between the rich and the poor and facilitates the evolution of a more balanced social and economic structure.

In countries where the relatively rich are politically powerful and have the capacity to pre-empt a larger proportion of future incomes and economic opportunities, even these intermediate solutions might not be practicable. In such countries certain partial solutions may perhaps work through the 'trickle-down' effects of agricultural progress in the form of larger employment opportunities or of facilities for small farmers. But in the longer run the income-distribution patterns and the nature of social relationships will continue to worsen.

The need to pay greater attention to the agricultural sector is no longer a matter of debate. Even though the rural population accounts for 50-90 per cent of the total population in most developing countries, the agricultural sector in these countries is receiving no more than 18-20 per cent of total investment. Most of the economic policies also adversely affect the agriculture sector and often squeeze out resources from it through exchange-rate policies or fiscal devices. One of the important lessons of the Chinese experience is its emphasis on agricultural investment and improvement which only in due course provides the basis for modern industry. This is very different from the strategy of concentrating most of the investment in modern industry and in the urban areas in the hope that the spill-over effects will somehow reach the rural areas.

Sustained agricultural progress can relieve rural poverty to some extent because of larger employment opportunities and more food at reasonable prices, but it will not automatically solve the income-distribution problem. As the experience of the past twenty-five years clearly shows, the large and medium farmers, with more land and better access to credit, technology and markets, pre-empt a much larger proportion of those benefits. If more food is produced by the rich farmer, then the income disparities continue to grow and the contradictions between the rich and the poor become more antagonistic. At least one intermediate step towards the goal of reducing rural poverty can be taken by adopting a strategy of development which is concentrated on the small farmer and is supported by a rapid expansion of social services in rural areas.

But a strategy of rural development focused on the small

farmer will not by itself solve the problems of the landless workers and their families who constitute 15–20 per cent of the rural population in many developing countries and the hard core of the rural poor. If the pace of agricultural development is rapid and if social services in the rural areas are expanding, a proportion of the landless workers will be drawn into the employment stream and the dire poverty of this group will be relieved to some extent. But the ultimate objective of rural development should be to end the marginal existence of this segment of the rural population and integrate them as full and equal members of the rural community. This cannot, however, be accomplished unless they have some access to land and other resources in the rural areas and that is where the political obstacles to rural development reach their maximum complexity. Only eight developing countries have on the average more than 2 hectares of arable land for every rural inhabitant; in fifty-two of them, the area is less than 1 hectare per capita. Possibilities of industrial and urban employment are limited in most developing countries and the rate of population growth is creating further pressure on available land. In such a situation, the lot of the landless and the rural poor cannot be improved without a major redistribution of land and other assets, and that cannot be achieved without a direct or indirect shift in the political power structure in favour of the poor.

Thus the only long-term and viable solution to the problem of rural poverty is a comprehensive approach to the rural development in which land and other rural resources can be distributed equally or at least equitably, followed by a gradual process of collectivisation and then the diversification of the rural economy. These three elements of the strategy can be further strengthened by an improvement in the structure of social relationships that is based on the collective spirit and the principle of equality of opportunity and by a political system committed to improve the lot of the poor majority.

The social existence of man has presented him with different choices at different times to solve his problems and no solution can provide satisfactory answers to all the problems for an indefinite period of time. But at this particular juncture in man's history, the lessons of the Chinese experience can hardly be ignored.

Appendix A

Comparative Statement on the Availability of Arable Land in Developing and Developed Countries

ASIA

Country	Total population ('ooos)	Agricultural population ('ooos)	Arable land ('ooo ha)	Arable land per capita for agric. pop. (ha/person)
	1	2	3	4
Mongolia	1,248	772	801	1.04
Burma	27,748	16,529	9,973	0.60
Afghanistan	16,978	13,866	7,920	0.57
Malaysia	10,466	5,810	3,339	0.57
Pakistan	60,449	35,577	19,450[1]	0.55
Khymer Republic	7,060	5,519	2,900	0.53
Thailand	35,745	28,552	12,500	0.44
India	543,132	376,603	160,700	0.43
Laos People's Dem. Rep.	2,962	2,334	960[1]	0.41
Philippines	37,604	20,194	7,580	0.38
Dem. Korean Rep.	13,892	7,598	2,100[1]	0.28
China, People's Rep.	771,840	522,950	130,000[1]	0.25
Nepal	11,232	10,544	2,000[1]	0.19
Dem. Rep. of Vietnam	39,106	29,889	5,500[1]	0.18
Indonesia	119,467	79,160	13,300	0.17
Bangladesh	67,692	58,146	8,900*	0.15
Rep. of Korea	31,365	15,995	2,238	0.14
Sri Lanka	12,522	6,904	895	0.13

NEAR AND MIDDLE EAST

Country	Total population	Agricultural population	Arable land	Arable land per capita
Syrian Arab Rep.	6,247	3,193	5,682	1.78
Jordan	2,280	769	1,170	1.52
Iran	28,359	13,048	15,700	1.20
Iraq	9,356	4,360	5,100	1.17
Turkey	35,232	23,865	25,128	1.05
Lebanon	2,469	484	240*	0.50
Yemen Dem. Rep.	1,436	927	334*[1]	0.36
Yemen Arab Rep.	5,767	4,568	1,240[1]	0.27
Saudi Arabia	7,740	5,109	700	0.14

AFRICA

Country	Total population ('000s)	Agricultural population ('000s)	Arable land ('000 ha)	Arable land per capita for agric. pop. (ha/person)
	1	2	3	4
Niger	4,016	3,728	15,000[1]	4.02
Libyan Arab Rep.	1,938	622	2,400	3.86
Mali	5,047	4,592	11,700[1]	2.55
Benin	2,686	1,337	2,950[1]	2.21
Ivory Coast	4,310	3,642	8,000	2.20
Chad	3,740	3,283	7,000*[1]	2.13
Sierra Leone	2,644	1,890	3,670	1.94
Zambia	4,295	3,127	4,985[1]	1.59
Togo	1,960	1,437	2,220	1.54
Cameroon	5,836	4,960	6,750	1.36
Tunisia	5,137	2,562	3,200	1.25
Guinea	3,921	3,321	4,150[1]	1.25
Upper Volta	5,384	4,671	5,315*	1.14
Tanzania	13,273	11,437	11,150	0.97
Morocco	15,126	8,598	7,180	0.84
Senegal	3,925	3,128	2,300*	0.74
Algeria	14,330	8,702	6,400	0.74
Malawi	4,360	3,895	2,895[1]	0.74
Nigeria	55,073	34,230	25,300[1]	0.74
Rhodesia	5,038	3,389	2,480[1]	0.73
Ethiopia	24,855	20,906	13,000*	0.62
Sudan	15,695	12,871	7,150	0.56
Madagascar	6,932	6,195	2,950[1]	0.48
Mozambique	8,234	6,089	2,850	0.47
Uganda	9,806	8,428	3,900	0.46
Zaire	21,638	17,258	7,750[1]	0.45
Somalia	2,789	2,362	1,040	0.44
Burundi	3,350	2,919	1,070	0.37
Angola	5,670	3,626	1,310[1]	0.36
Ghana	8,628	5,042	1,050	0.21
Rwanda	3,679	3,431	659	0.19
Kenya	11,247	9,236	1,570	0.17
Egypt	33,329	18,125	2,724	0.15

LATIN AMERICA

Country	Total population ('000s)	Agricultural population ('000s)	Arable land ('000 ha)	Arable land per capita for agric. pop. (ha/person)
	1	2	3	4
Argentina	23,748	3,885	24,620	6.34
Uruguay	2,955	448	1,810	4.04
Chile	9,369	2,225	5,550	2.49
Venezuela	10,559	2,700	4,750	1.76
Cuba	8,565	2,621	3,720[1]	1.42
Bolivia	4,780	2,655	3,135	1.18
Mexico	50,313	22,751	25,620	1.13
Ecuador	6,031	3,069	3,224*	1.05
Puerto Rico	2,743	223	200[1]	0.90
Nicaragua	1,970	967	790	0.82
Panama	1,458	606	440	0.73
Paraguay	2,301	1,212	810	0.67
Brazil	95,204	43,432	28,000	0.64
Honduras	2,553	1,995	870[1]	0.51
Jamaica	1,882	553	260[1]	0.47
Peru	13,248	5,938	2,600	0.44
Colombia	22,075	8,356	3,620	0.43
Guatemala	5,298	3,231	1,370	0.42
Costa Rica	1,737	731	290	0.40
Trinidad & Tobago	955	179	70	0.39
Dominican Rep.	4,343	2,660	645	0.25
Haiti	4,235	3,263	525	0.16

DEVELOPED COUNTRIES

Country	Total population ('000s)	Agricultural population ('000s)	Arable land ('000 ha)	Arable land per capita for agric. pop. (ha/person)
	1	2	3	4
Australia	12,510	1,012	44,800	44.27
The United States	204,879	7,525	205,080*	27.25
Canada	21,406	1,762	43,100[1]	24.46
Denmark	4,929	550	2,641	4.80
The United Kingdom	55,480	1,555	7,078	4.55

DEVELOPED COUNTRIES (*contd*)

Country	Total population ('ooos)	Agricultural population ('ooos)	Arable land ('ooo ha)	Arable land per capita for agric. pop. (ha/person)
	1	2	3	4
The Soviet Union	242,768	62,288	227,800	3.66
Finland	4,606	981	2,654	2.71
France	50,770	6,959	17,235	2.48
New Zealand	2,820	334	820	2.46
Czechoslovakia	14,339	2,424	5,161	2.13
German Dem. Rep.	17,058	2,216	4,663	2.10
Hungary	10,338	2,586	5,129	1.98
Spain	33,615	8,736	15,918	1.82
Belgium	9,638	467	795	1.70
Norway	3,877	461	780	1.69
German Fed. Rep.	60,700	4,527	7,553	1.67
Austria	7,391	1,096	1,514	1.38
Ireland	2,954	783	1,050*	1.34
Israel	2,910	283	342	1.21
Poland	32,473	12,669	14,764	1.17
Portugal	8,628	2,875	3,050	1.06
Bulgaria	8,490	3,958	4,098	1.04
Italy	53,660	10,076	9,319	0.92
Romania	20,244	11,336	9,703	0.86
Greece	8,793	3,786	2,980	0.79
Switzerland	6,190	484	366	0.76
Netherlands	13,032	1,059	799	0.75
Yugoslavia	20,371	10,143	7,355	0.73
Japan	104,331	20,501	4,978	0.24

SOURCE OF DATA IN APPENDIX A

1. All *data* and *definitions* are taken from the *FAO Production Yearbook 1975*, vol. 29. Unless indicated all data have been supplied by the countries listed. Estimates of total and agricultural population and total available arable land. *FAO Production Yearbook 1975*, vol. 29, pp. 35—8 and pp. 3—23 respectively.
2. Population estimates refer to 1970; estimates for arable land refer to 1974.
3. All data on arable land are based on FAO data for 1974.
   Unofficial figures are marked *.
   [1]Denotes arable land and land under permanent crops combined.

Appendix B
Statistical Information on forty-one Communes

Name of commune	Province	Population	Cultivated/ irrigated area (hectares)	Average yield of crops (tons/ hectare)	Average yearly income/head (Yuan)	Non-agric. employ-ment	Non-agric. income	Educa-tional facili-ties	Health facili-ties	Other signifi-cant features	Source	Year figures given
Peking Municipality												
Louchang	Peking Municipality	14,456 15PB 45PT	2,012	R6.01	272 (+260kg grain)	200		21P; 1LM;	15 HC	11F; 11T; 38HT; 2TR; 86PS	Henle p. 216	1971
Sungchiao	Peking Municipality	40,000 6PB 59PT	3,577	W5.3	130 (+275kg grain)		50%	19P;6UM;	1 H;6HC	15F	FAO Mission Item 5 Henle, p. 213	1975 1971
Marco Polo Bridge	Peking Municipality	41,000 5PB 146PT	2,300 100%					24P; 2M;	5 HC	8T; 23HT; 42TR	Oldham	1963
Red Star	Peking Municipality	80,000	10,850	R5.7				69P; 10M;	1 H	15T; 250HT; 30TR;	Current Scene, Jan 1976, vol. 14, No. 1	1973
China-Korea Friendship	Municipality									68,000A; 1,000PW		
Huang tu-kang	Peking Municipality	34,000	3,000 95%		147		3M	1 H; 11HC		41,000A; 600PW; 53HT; 20T; 50TR	Obaidullah	1970

Name of commune	Province	Population	Cultivated/ irrigated area (hectares)	Average yield of crops (tons/ hectare)	Average yearly income/head (Yuan)	Non-agric. employment	Non-agric. income	Educational facilities	Health facilities	Other significant features	Source	Year figures given
Shanghai Municipality												
Huang tu	Shanghai Municipality	23,000 16PB 133PT	2,100 100%	V85 G13.5	207		>50%	23P; 7LM; 16 HC 2UM		10F; 25T; 33HT; 140FM	FAO Mission Item 25	1974
Tang Wan	Shanghai Municipality	20,170 12PB 128PT	1,786 97%	G5.3 C2.03	330			21P; 1LM	1 H; 3 HC	7T; 3HT	Oldham	1963
Horse Bridge	Shanghai Municipality	35,000	90%	G12.35 C0.9					1 H	T C 49,000A	Current Scene, Jan 1976, vol. 14, No. 1	1975
July 1st	Shanghai Municipality	17,000 11PB 88PT	4,122 90%	C1.1 C0.75	190	1,100 (11%)			1 H	T C 20,000A	Current Scene, Jan 1976, vol. 14, No. 1	1973
Ma Lu	Shanghai Municipality	28,000 14PB 144PT	2,261 95%	G13.95 C0.68	200	15.3%	30%	24P; 10M	1 H; 14HC	190T + HT; 27PS	Author's own notes	1975
South-east Region												
Huatung	Kuangtung	59,287 20PB 319PT	4,740	R8.44	456/household	3,670	22%	31P; 3LM; 1H; 20HC 1UM		22T; 201HT; 15F	Moorehouse Henle, p. 259	1972
Fucheng	Kuangtung	41,760 8PB 109PT	3,370	R11.8 K10.9	695/household (+330kg grain)			32P; 3LM; 1H; 8HC 1UM		34F; 13T; 45HT; 5TR; 42,000A	Henle, p. 263	1971
Sachiao	Kuangtung	70,000 25PB 311PT	4,067	R9.7 SU8.1 SC1.8	304 (+260kg grain)	9,000	20%	24P; 3LM; 1H 1UM		9PS; 48,000A	FAO Mission Item 38	1973
Yan Buh	Kuangtung	60,300 12PB 202PT	2,453	R8.8 298				47P; 4M	2H; 12HC	10T; 5F; 42PS	Henle, p. 252 Oldham, op. cit. 1963	1972
Hsinhua.	Kuangtung	64,500 21PB 321PT	5,400	R8.0	725/household					6F; 33PS; 220T + HT	Author's own notes	1972
Da Li	Kuangtung	63,000 19PB 237PT	4,000	R9.9	– (+365kg grain)		25%				Dickenson, Chinese Rural Development, Univ. of Edinburgh	1972

Name of commune	Province	Population	Cultivated/ irrigated area (hectares)	Average yield of crops (tons/ hectare)	Average yearly income/head (Yuan)	Non-agric. employment	Non-agric. income	Educational facilities	Health facilities	Other significant features	Source	Year figures given
Southeast Region (contd)												
Yanhsi	Fukien	29,000 10PB 146PT	3,070 80%	G9.0	103	3,000 (25%)		59P; 1M	1H	53T; 100 + FM	China Reconstructs (Dec. 1973)	1972
Chiangh-siang	Kiangsi	53,000	6,900	G6.0	Doubled since 1957					55PS; 30T; 2TR; 600B; 9G	NCNA 17.10.73	1972
Northern Region												
Chiliying	Honan	55,000 38PB 298PT	6,300 91%	G8.3 C1.2	140	400		38P; 17M	1H; 38HC	44F; 102T + HT	Inside a People's Commune, Foreign Lang. Press, Peking	1973
Huikuo chen	Honan	58,000 21PB 211PT	3,266	G7.62	160	3,212				74F; 9TR; 149T + HT	People's Daily, 11.11.75	1974
Chentsun	Hopei	20,000 9PB 70PT	2,800	G6.2							China Features Peking	1972
Chienming	Hopei	14,500 21PB 59PT	1,290	G6.0				21P; 6M			Peking Review, Nos. 51 and 52 (1974)	1973
Wang Mang	Shensi		1,600 50%	G4.65			40%			18T; 1TR; 60FM; 13,000A	NCNA 10.4.74	1973
Kung-pengtze	Kirin	27,000 11PB 77PT	7,716	G4.35	4.5 times 1958 figures	20%	55%			45T; 390FM; 21,500A	NCNA 21.9.73	1972
Peiyuan	Shantung	2,500	G3.5 times up on 1957 Vo.5 times up on 1957							43F; 94T	Peking Review, No.34 23.8.74	1973

Northern Region (contd)

Name of commune	Province	Population	Cultivated/irrigated area (hectares)	Average yield of crops (tons/hectare)	Average yearly income/head (Yuan)	Non-agric. employment	Non-agric. income	Educational facilities	Health facilities	Other significant features	Source	Year figures given
Hsiating-chia	Shantung	4,000 households 22PB	1,000 66%	G doubled since 1958	Up 2.5 times since 1958 (+235kg grain)					44PS	NCNA 30.9.73	1972
Tachai	Shansi	11,100 21PB	1,200 40%	G6.88			25%			17PS; 32T + TR	NCNA 5.10.73	1971
Eastern Region												
Holei	Kiangsu	15,100 7PB 87PT		W5.6 R9.4	148				1H	2T;80HT; 4TR; 146FM; 25PS; 11B	FAO Mission Item 21	1974
Changchin	Kiangsu	19,342 15PB 161PT	1,038	G12.1	149 (+248kg grain)		29.4%	19P; 1M	1H	15F; 75T; 2HT; TC; 72oB; 21,000A		
October	Kiangsu	10,354 7PB 89PT	717		750/household			9P; 3M	1H; 4HC	5F; 4TR; No T	Oldham op. cit.	1963
Tungting	Kiangsu	45,000 30PB 237PT			133	500		36P; 8M	1H	15F; 24T; 600FM	Report from Tungting, Foreign Lang. Press (1975)	1973
Yuehsi	Kiangsu	12,000		G12.9	145 (+250kg grain) 3 fold increase over 1957			1M		TC; 14PS; 10F; 900FM	NCNA 27.9.74	1973
Chaoyang	Kiangsu	11,300 65PT	920							35T; 9E; 230FM	NCNA 21.8.73	1972
Fotzuling	Anhwei	640 86%	R6.4		858/household					4T + TR 21EM	NCNA 16.10.73	1972
Chienchiao	Chekiang	21,909 24PB 283PT	1,111 86%	G6.86 J3.8 Vo.79				17P; 1M	1H	No T; 28PS	Oldham op.cit.	1963

Name of commune	Province	Population	Cultivated/ irrigated area (hectares)	Average yield of crops (tons/ hectare)	Average yearly income/head (Yuan)	Non-agric. employ-ment	Non-agric. income	Educa-tional facili-ties	Health facili-ties	Other signifi-cant features	Source	Year figures given
Central Region												
Liuchi	Hupeh	13,200 6PB 73PT	880 100%	G12 C1.43	— (+275kg grain)	1,160 (20%)	40%	6P; 1M	1H; 6HC	13F; 66T; 5TR; 530FM 13E	NCNA 24.10.75	1974
Shaoshan	Hunan	13,000 9PB 80PT	80%	G8.1							NCNA 21.10.73	1972
Minority Nationality Communes												
Red Star	Sinkiang A.R.	18,000 9PB	6,000							90,000A; 40TR + T; 80FM	China Reconstructs (Dec. 1975)	1974
Hsinngo	Heilungkiang	600	460		210					3F; 4T; 20M	China Reconstructs (Feb. 1973)	1971
Tungwang	Yunnan	5,000 40PT	660 70%	G3.9	10-20% increase/year					27,000A	NCNA 28.8.73	1972
Chaka	Chinghai	1,564 2PB 6PT	260	G3.0						81,000A	NCNA 11.9.73	1972

NOTES: The absence of figures in any column denotes that the information is not available.

1. *Population:* PB = Production Brigade; PT = Production Team
2. *Average yield of crops:* G = Grain; V = Vegetables; C = Cotton; R = Rice; W = Wheat; K = Kaoling; J = Jute; SU = Sugar; SC = Silk Cocoons.
3. *Average yearly income/head* means per capita cash distribution; where figures are available, the yearly amount of grain distributed is also given.
4. *Non-agricultural employment* includes commune members working in local industries and agricultural sideline activities.
5. *Non-agricultural income* is the collective income from industrial and agricultural sideline activities expressed as a percentage of the commune's gross income from all sources.
6. *Educational facilities:* P = Primary; LM = Lower Middle; M = Middle; UM = Upper Middle.
7. *Health facilities:* H = Hospital; HC = Health Clinic.
8. *Other significant features:* F = Factory; TR = Truck; T = Tractor; HT = Hand Tractor; TC = Triple Cropping; FM = Farm Machinery; PS = Pumping Station; A = Animals; E = Enterprises; M = Motors; EM = Engines and Motors; B = Boats; PW = Pump Wells'

Sources: FAO, *Professional Study Mission to China* (September 1975) unpublished notes C. G. H. Oldham, unpublished data collected on private visits to the PRC in 1964 and 1965, NCNA: New China News Agency. Henle, *Report on China's Agriculture*, FAO (1974).

Obaidullah, *The Yellow Sand Hills*, Bangladesh Academy for Rural Development, Comilla, Bangladesh (1975). Moorehouse, Unpublished report on 1973 visit to the PRC, New York University.

Appendix C

Some Other Experiments in Rural Development

Different countries have experimented with different approaches to rural development in the past thirty years with varying results. This chapter reviews these approaches in a few selected countries in the light of the criteria suggested in Chapter 6 to judge the efficacy and results of these efforts in achieving one or more objectives of rural development.

Economic objectives, assessed in terms of average growth rates in agriculture or productivity per acre or per worker are an important component of a strategy of rural development and are necessary for achieving social and political objectives of rural development but, as the experience of the past two decades clearly shows, economic progress in industry or agriculture will not by itself ensure improved income distribution or growing employment opportunities. In fact, in pure economic terms the overall record of developing countries in agriculture is not all that bad. Taken as a group, they have managed an average annual increase of about 3 per cent in agricultural production in the past twenty-five years since 1950, which is better than the average growth rate achieved by the United States, Europe and even Japan in the first twenty-five years of their agricultural modernisation. But their population growth in this period was twice as fast (2 – 2.5 per cent per annum) and, more important, the benefits of this progress have not been evenly distributed. It is only when one goes beyond average growth rates to broader objectives of rural development that one begins to realise the real difference between agricultural and rural development.

Any meaningful assessment of the results of a particular development strategy, notwithstanding the mixture of objectives chosen by the country itself, must include answers to at least a few key questions:

- What are the results of the strategy in economic and technological terms, and increments in total output and output per man or per acre?
- What has been the effect on the employment situation and on income distribution?
- What has been the impact on the poorest segments of the rural population and in meeting their basic needs?
- Has the rural community acquired or increased its capacity, administrative, technical and financial, to diversify the rural economy?
- Has the rural community been able, with whatever help is available from the State, to build rural infrastructure and to provide certain essential social services?

The assessment presented here includes only a few selected cases in which the countries concerned have either achieved notable success or whose experience would seem to offer some interesting lessons or insights into the problems or prospects of rural development.

JAPAN

Japan is generally cited as one of the most successful examples of agricultural development in which a very efficient pattern of technological change has been evolved on small farms after the Meiji Restoration of 1868. Japan's resource endowment at that time was not different from that of many developing countries of today – a surplus of agricultural labour and shortage of land and capital.[1] Japan's agriculture was subject to heavy taxation from 1870 to 1913 and, in fact, Japan's industrial investment in the initial phases was largely financed out of the surplus produced by agriculture, yet Japan achieved a sustained increase in agricultural productivity on essentially small-scale privately-owned farms.

A great deal has already been written about Japan's agricultural development and agricultural policy to analyse the main factors that contributed to this success.[2] These include, apart from initial access to improved technology, higher (70 per cent) literacy in 1870 and a tradition of hard work and discipline:

- the active role of central government to support land reclamation and agricultural research and training;
- the work of prefectoral administration in testing, spreading and often enforcing new seeds and better farming techniques;
- the sense of solidarity among farmers living in a village with collective responsibility for tax payment and backed by various forms of co-operative activity such as communal farming, co-operative glass houses, co-operative livestock breeding and communal direction for farms cultivated on a family basis;
- the paternalistic authority of the landlord and his interest in improving his tenants' land and income;
- the innovative role of the capitalist entrepreneurs and the individual Japanese farmer, particularly in new rice varieties, use of organic fertilizer and crop diversification.[3]

The rate of agricultural production in Japan, however, slowed down during the inter-war period, from an average of about 2 per cent in 1870–1913 to less than 1 per cent in 1919–39. This has been ascribed partly to technological factors and partly to economic factors. The initial group of innovators were owner cultivators operating 2–5 hectares of land but their profits began to decline because of higher labour costs after the First World War. With increased imports of cheap rice from abroad during the interim period, the terms of trade generally moved against the agricultural sector. The impact of the initial technological changes without any consciously induced institutional changes also affected the overall productivity of agriculture.[4] After the Second World War, however, there was another land reform and Japan's agricultural productivity jumped sharply with a massive increase in the supply of chemical fertilizer and agricultural machinery. The shift of agricultural labour to non-agricultural sectors also accelerated considerably in this period and facilitated the process of mechanisation and modernisation. Japan has achieved yields of 6–7 tons of rice per hectare which is two to three times that in most developing countries.

If Japan's agricultural and rural development policy is

assessed in terms of the criteria proposed earlier, the most important lesson of Japan's experience is that there is nothing inherently unproductive in a small farm, provided some collective or co-operative arrangements can be made through Government or communal efforts to provide credit, farm inputs and modern technology. Japan's initial success was largely due to the elimination of the feudal system of land-holding and the subsequent innovative role of the Japanese farmers supported by Government and by wide ranging co-operative activities. It also succeeded in organising the traditional rural community to control and manage available water resources on a collective basis and provided supplementary irrigation to a very high proportion of its cultivated area. This has been a very important factor in increasing rice yields in Japan.

The second important lesson of the Japanese experience is its success in mobilising resources for modernising agriculture from within the agricultural sector. Despite sizeable agricultural taxation (which was largely possible because even before the Meiji Restoration the Japanese farmer was paying up to 40 per cent of his net income to the landlord), the Government did not neglect the agricultural sector. A massive effort to improve and spread new techniques, better seeds and fertilizers was launched during this period and a great deal of the increase in production was reinvested by the innovating farmers.

But Japan was not able to absorb continuing additions to the rural labour force while increasing agricultural productivity, as most contemporary developing countries have to. In Japan the employment problem did not become serious because of a very rapid and sustained increase in industrial activity, which was particularly rapid after the Second World War. Japan's rural population therefore declined from 65 per cent in 1870 to 42 per cent in 1939 and about 22 per cent in 1970 with a corresponding growth in urban population. Japan thus avoided the problem of rural unemployment but is now facing serious problems of urbanisation.

Another social objective in respect of which Japan's success was partial was that of income distribution. While between 1870 and 1913, Japan was able to improve the income of its rural population, particularly the poorest among them, it was not able to prevent a widening inequality between urban and rural incomes. This forced the Government to launch somewhat belatedly a price-support operation in agriculture. The budgetary cost of this programme to the Government became particularly heavy after the Second World War. There were also certain avoidable distortions in agricultural prices. For example, the domestic support price of rice in the early 1970s, before the recent increases in world grain prices, was four to five times the world market price of rice.

Japan's success in achieving significant agricultural progress has thus many important lessons for land-scarce countries. It shows clearly that small private farms can be quite productive in terms of yield, provided the small farmers have access to credit and other inputs through their own co-operative or government agencies. But the Japanese experience is not as relevant for those developing countries which have to increase agricultural productivity while absorbing a growing population in agriculture, nor in relation to the objective of more equitable distribution of incomes within rural areas and as between urban and rural areas.

ISRAEL'S KIBBUTZ AND MOSHAV

Israel's kibbutz, and to some extent moshav, offers another successful example of collective farming, besides China, in which land is collectively owned, income is equally distributed, largely through improved services and facilities in kind, and the activities of the collective are not confined to agriculture. It also illustrates the importance of collective and co-operative efforts in the development of water resources and in sharing improved technology. Like China, ideological motivation has been an important factor in the success of the kibbutz, although the nature of the ideological and non-material motivation is of a very different kind.

Kibbutzim were first set up by immigrants in Palestine in the early part of this century and are based on the collective ownership of resources and an equal sharing of labour and farm produce amongst the members. On the average, a kibbutz has 300–400 members and a cultivated area of 200–1000 hectares.[5]

Members are provided with a small house but they have their food in a communal dining hall and, in most kibbutzim, children live together in nurseries and special quarters. Farming is managed and operated as a single unit, each member working according to a centralised work schedule. No wages are paid but members are provided with goods and services they need, with equal rights for all. Mixed farming is most commonly practised, with six to ten different branches over the years. Profits are not distributed among the members but are reinvested in the improvement of farm technology and the standard of social services. Although kibbutzim are primarily agricultural in character, many of them have introduced agricultural processing and industrial plants as an additional source of income.

The highest authority of the kibbutz is the General Assembly of all members, but the power is delegated to the elected committees at the village and the regional level for all purposes of planning and development and investment decisions. Only the major issues such as the decision on budget and annual election to committees are placed before the General Assembly.[6]

Moshav, which is another kind of rural settlement in Israel, is a co-operative of small-holding family farms, generally consisting of 80–100 farm units. As in the kibbutz, land belongs to the State but, unlike the kibbutz, the settler is allocated about 40 dunams of land (1 dunam = 0.1 hectare) on lease. Also, he owns the house and the inventory and, more important, the decisions on the pattern of farming and the mode of his consumption are left entirely to him; but at the same time, his economic and social security is ensured by the village co-operative, which provides all the inputs on a credit basis, handles the marketing of the farm produce and also provides social services like education and health.

On arrival in the village, the settler is provided with a house and is also allocated about 4 dunams of land (out of the 40 dunams which will be ultimately given to him) for growing vegetables, and the remaining area is managed as a large administered farm on which he is employed as a labourer. As he gains the farming knowledge and experience, his holding is gradually enlarged. In this way, the settlers are ensured of a stable income from the beginning without having to assume the risks of wasteful investments as a result of inexperienced management.[7]

The main difference between a kibbutz and a moshav is in the nature of organisation and management. A kibbutz is a unit of production, consumption and socialisation. It is a voluntary association of individuals but all have equal status in which members are paid in kind and through the expansion of social services. It is a way of life with a sense of community. A moshav is an association of households and not individuals, in which ownership of land is private and so is income, although many services including credit and marketing are provided by the moshav. Unlike kibbutzim, whose main purpose was development on socialist principles, moshavim were border settlements based on individual farmsteads. They brought together immigrants from a particular geographical or cultural background who were generally non-agriculturalists and were gradually trained to undertake cultivation. While the kibbutzim are much more autonomous in their management and have provided many political leaders to the country as a whole, moshavim are more tightly controlled by the Government and have played a less important political role.

Since the early 1950s, the moshav kind of settlement has been comparatively more popular among the settlers than the kibbutz. The growth of kibbutzim and moshavim between 1948 and 1970 is shown in Table C1. The major explanation for the more rapid growth of moshav is that the majority of new settlers have preferred the private ownership of property and freedom in farming and consumption decisions.

Before 1948 a mixed-farming system based on three main branches – dairy, poultry and vegetables – was commonly practised. But the simultaneous establishment of many villages on the mixed-farming pattern resulted in a market saturation for these products and, consequently, the rural development policies began to emphasise specialised farming and more intensive use of mechanical implements. Gradually, larger land units became necessary to facilitate future mechanisation. To meet this, the pattern of rural settlement was modified – the area adjacent to the habitat was reduced to 1 hectare or even less, and the rest of the land was sub-divided into several large plots, representing a unit of land adapted to branch specialisation, co-operative utilisation of machinery and aerial spraying.

Following a continuous increase in farm productivity, while at the same time a general slackening in the growth of domestic demand for agricultural output, rural development policies since

Table C1 Growth of kibbutzim and
moshavim during 1948–70

	Kibbutzim			Moshavim		
	1948[1]	1964[2]	1970[3]	1948[1]	1964[2]	1970[3]
1. No. of settlements	177	230	284[6]	104[7]	346	355
2. Population of these settlements	54,208	80,939	85,100	30,142	119,923	122,700
3. Percentage of total population	7.89	3.20	2.84	4.39	4.75	4.09
4. Percentage of total rural population	48.99	15.94	16.26	27.25	23.63	23.44
5. Cultivated area under kibbutzim ('000 hectares)	75.4[4]	136.1[5]	153.3	–	–	102.1
6. Percentage of total cultivated area	45.70[4]	34.28[5]	39.72	–	–	26.45

Sources: 1. Unesco, *Arid Zone Research, No. 23* (1964) p. 54.
2. E. Kanovsky, *The Economy of the Kibbutz* (Harvard: Harvard University, Middle Eastern Monograph No. 13, 1966) p. 9.
3. *Statistical Abstracts of Israel, 1974*.
4. These figures refer to the year 1949.
5. These figures refer to the year 1963.
6. The figure for kibbutzim in 1970 includes collective moshavim, that is, moshavim-shitufi.
7. The figure for moshavim in 1948 includes moshavim-shitufiym and private moshavim.

the early 1960s have come to emphasise:

(a) the improvement in the standard of social services at the village and regional level, thereby eliminating the economic, social and cultural gap between the town and the countryside;

(b) the use of new technologies and production techniques by

pooling resources together through regional co-operation;
(c) the establishment of agro-processing industries under collective ownership and management;
(d) the integration of agriculture, industry and services at the regional level;
(e) the shift to high-value crops like dairy products, fruit and vegetables, cotton and groundnuts with an optimal rotation of crops.

In early 1962 a special Rural Settlement Authority was set up with the responsibility for overall rural settlement. The Authority is highly decentralised, with the power delegated right down to the village and regional level. Planning and implementation are carried out in the regional offices, comprising interdisciplinary teams living in the region. The team works in close co-operation with local farmers' organisation and co-ordinates development activities with various departments at the regional and local level.

The collective and co-operative structure of farming, the provisions governing land tenure, more intensive use of available water supplies, the strong institutional support including an intensive extension service, the provision of credit, inputs and marketing facilities, effective price policies guaranteeing the minimum prices and insurance coverage against bad harvests have resulted in both a high rate of growth of agricultural output – an average annual rate of 8.8 per cent[8] – and an equitable distribution of the benefits among the farmers. Also, the emphasis on the integration of agriculture, industry and services and the development of agro-processing and industrial plants under collective ownership and management has considerably expanded the employment opportunities in rural areas, while at the same time the surplus income created by these industries has remained within the rural areas.

The rate of growth of agricultural output in the kibbutz has been somewhat faster than the agricultural sector as a whole, but the proportion of rural population outside the collective sector has been increasing at a faster rate. The decline in the proportion of rural population in the kibbutzim has been particularly rapid.

If Israel's experience is carefully analysed in relation to the criteria mentioned in Chapter 6 the results are remarkably impressive. Starting with immigrants who had little experience with agriculture, the rural settlements achieved rapid and sustained increment in agricultural production. In terms of social objectives, the distribution of income and social facilities within the rural communities has been fairly equitable and the capacity of political and administrative systems to provide leadership and guidance to rural communities and in linking their needs and production with the rest of the economy has been very effective. Israel's experience with collective and co-operative farming under two different models also highlights their success in organising collective ownership of the land, co-operative services and opportunities for diversification to non-agricultural activities. The system did not permit exploitation of one class by another and yet provided freedom to those settlers who wanted to leave the settlement and move to the cities.

Like China, Israel's experience has many unique features, but it also demonstrates that ideological and non-material motivation required for creating a more egalitarian or socialist society is not necessarily tied to only one set of circumstances or one particular system.

BULGARIA

Bulgaria is one of the most successful examples of collective agriculture in East Europe.[9] Between 1956 and 1975, Bulgaria has achieved an annual average increase of 9 per cent in GNP, 4.5 per cent in agriculture and 12 per cent in industry.

The transformation of Bulgarian agriculture despite difficulties arising from a mountainous terrain and exposure to frequent floods has been very impressive. Within a relatively short period, peasants' small holdings were merged into co-operative farms and State farms were established on land belonging to the Government. By the end of 1969 there were 795 co-operative farms in Bulgaria with an average area of 4.100 hectares, in addition to 159 State farms which also had an average area of 4.000 hectares, altogether accounting for 99.5 per cent of all arable land in Bulgaria. By 1970 the Government felt the need for still larger units to facilitate further development of agriculture. These were formed by merging co-operative farms and State farms into 170 agro-industrial complexes. These agro-industrial complexes, supported by twelve State enterprises responsible for all bulk purchasing and marketing of farm products, have been an important factor in Bulgaria's continued progress in agriculture. Present policies aim at a further enlargement of their size by merging these 170 agro-industrial complexes into about thirty organisations.

The average size of an agro-industrial complex (APK) is 24.000 hectares and they include 91 per cent of all arable land and 90 per cent of all rural labour force. The average population of one APK is about 7000. The main task of an APK is to specialise its production, expand mechanisation and chemicalisation of agriculture and increase and improve water control and utilisation. On the average, 40 per cent of APKs are expected to specialise in the production of grapes, 27 per cent in vegetables and 19 per cent in industrial crops such as cotton, rose and mint, but 90 per cent of them are also expected to produce grains and animal products. Half of APKs are communally-owned co-operatives, 42 per cent are mixed and 7 per cent are exclusively State organisations.

The internal organisation and management differs in certain aspects from one APK to another but, in a typical APK, all the adult workers elect delegates to a General Assembly which in turn elects, by secret ballot, an Executive Council, consisting of 'specialists' (generally about two-thirds) and 'ordinary workers'. The Executive Council elects a President who is assisted by four or five deputies, each in charge of a department and assisted by a chief specialist. Co-operative workers are organised into 'brigades' each headed by an agronomist or trained workers. Each worker, to secure his membership rights, is obliged to contribute a minimum number of days in a year: these range from 200–300 days in different APKs. The workers receive regular basic payment per day of work plus a share in the assessed annual profit of the APK, in addition to many goods and services in kind. Members are also entitled to retirement pension at the age of sixty and 15–18 days' paid holiday in a year.

Each worker is allowed to cultivate privately a small plot of land, generally about one-fifth of a hectare, and to keep some livestock. The produce of these plots can be sold through the co-operative shops or in the open markets. Villages have been largely reconstructed and workers usually own their houses.

Because of the rapid expansion of industrial activities, labour supply in rural areas has been dwindling. To tackle the problem, auxiliary brigades are formed by outside volunteers, students and office workers and assigned to different APKs for seasonal work.

As in other East European countries, the overall motivation in Bulgaria is increasingly dependent on economic incentives and rewards and less on ideological factors. This has led to certain problems of adjustments: demand for certain goods like housing and cars is greater than the supply. Despite policies to prevent serious imbalances in the distribution of incomes, the relatively higher-income group move into a different scale of consumption and the society as a whole seems to be moving away from the objective of building a 'classless society'. But the gap between the higher and lower-income groups is not large, there is no exploitation of any class or group of people in the system and opportunities for individual initiative and freedom of mobility and occupation are increasing.

In overall terms, Bulgaria is a very good example of combining co-operative and State farms into agro-industrial complexes which are large enough for large-scale mechanisation, widespread application of modern technology and setting up rural industries, and yet sufficiently decentralised and self-governing to give the members of the complexes a sense of participation. As a model of rural development, Bulgaria would seem to meet most of the criteria listed in Chapter 6.

TANZANIA

The purpose of society is man; but in order to serve man there must be a social organization of economic activities which is conducive to the greater production of things useful for the material and spiritual welfare of man. This means that it may well be a function of society to organize and sustain efficient economic organization and production techniques even when these are in themselves unpleasant or restrictive.

Mwalimu J. K. Nyrere

Tanzania's efforts to evolve a pattern of rural socialism based on the concept of ujamaa villages represent an outstanding example of a non-violent transition to an egalitarian and self-reliant, socio-economic system in which the primary emphasis is on organising a rural population to help themselves, first by building rural settlements to live together, then by providing essential social services for everyone and then gradually moving to collective farming and technical improvements in agriculture. Like China, Tanzania's primary emphasis has been on the social transformation and not only on agricultural growth. The experiment started only recently (1967) and it may be premature to evaluate and judge all its results, but as a pattern of rural development it already reveals some very interesting features and lessons.

For a few years after 1961, the year in which Tanzania achieved its independence, the focus of Government activity in rural areas was on the construction of highly-capitalised 'village settlements' in many parts of the country. But the results of these settlements which were based on a technocratic approach were not encouraging: they were expensive in terms of capital required and benefited only a small segment of the population.

The Arusha Declaration of 1967 marked a more radical approach to rural socialism based on the concept of ujamaa (co-operative) villages.[10] The basic strategy for rural development has been 'to farm village land collectively with modern techniques of production and to share the proceeds according to the work contributed. By building on the principles of the traditional extended family with its emphasis on co-operation and mutual respect and responsibility, a society will be built in which all members have equal rights and opportunities, where there is no exploitation of man by man and where all have a gradually increasing level of material life before any individual lives in luxury . . .'[11]

The establishment of an ujamaa village has usually been accomplished in three stages: 'villagisation' is obviously the first stage, whereby people are persuaded by the local and TANU officials to move from their houses, scattered over a wide area, into a single village and live together as a community, jointly enjoying the common facilities like schools, medical care and water supplies, which are normally built by the members themselves though with financial assistance from the Government. Next, the people are persuaded to start a small communal plot which will be jointly farmed and the proceeds jointly shared.

And finally, once the people have some confidence in the communal farming, they are persuaded to pool their land together, all the members working jointly according to the commonly accepted division of work.

The new approach emphasised the self-help principle and relegated 'commandism': 'It is vital that whatever encouragement government and TANU give to this type of scheme, they must not try to run it. They must help the people to run it.'[12]

The Second Five Year Plan also called for a 'frontal approach', i.e. 'moving towards ujamaa on all possible fronts to ensure that in the next five years, large segments of the society will make some movement towards socialism rather than a selective approach of providing a high level of service to a small number of ujamaa communities.'[13]

In 1973, TANU's National Congress determined that villagisation should be compulsory and set the end of 1976 as the target date for completing the exercise. The new villages were not necessarily to be ujamaa, i.e. villagisation was compulsory but not communal production. Village population increased from 2.6 million in 1974 to 9.1 million in 1975 and to 13.1 million in 1976 (see Table C2). Despite some cases of 'commandism' and

Table C2 Progress of villagisation in Tanzania

	Villages*	Population of ujamaa villages	Total population ('ooos)	Rural population	Ujamaa (as % total)	Population (as % rural pop.)
1971	4484	1,545,240	13,630	12,415	11.4	12.5
1973	5626	2,028,164	14,380	13,176	14.1	15.4
1974	5008	2,560,472	14,760	13,500	17.4	19.0
1975*	6944	9,140,229	15,160	13,780	60.3	66.3
1976*	7658	13,067,220	15,580	14,080	83.9	92.8

* Ujamaa and development villages.
Source: *Vijiji Vilivyoshinda Saba Saba 1976* (Prime Minister's Office, Dodoma, Tanzania, 1976).

more of ill-prepared moves, the exercise did succeed in grouping more than 90 per cent of the rural population in communities. While the sharp 1975 and 1976 increases in food output are probably largely attributable to better weather, ujamaa villages are helping to create better conditions for future progress in agriculture. The 1975 legislation has reinforced village land rights, created guidelines for community self-government and production management and provided substantial powers for elected village councils.

The transition towards communal farming has been very promising in some regions. For example, in Horohoro (Tonga region) and in Idete and Lukenge (Morogoro region), communal farming has been accepted universally and all crops including cash crops are owned and cultivated communally and the proceeds jointly shared. In some regions, where the proportion of cash crops like coffee, tea, cotton and tobacco is larger, individual farms have been more successful and it is difficult to persuade them to join the communal system of farming. But there are very few large landowners in Tanzania. Over 83 per cent of total cultivated land (4.40 million hectares in 1973) was in holdings below 2 hectares, with 31.5 per cent in holdings below 0.5 hectares.[14] This structure of land-ownership has been a positive factor and should greatly facilitate further progress towards the objective of communal farming.

From 1967–75 the inequality between urban and rural wages increased at about the same rate. The ujamaa villages have generally been concentrated on the poorest segments of the rural population and have therefore helped to alleviate rural poverty by creating conditions which allows every able-bodied Tanzanian to earn enough to meet minimum acceptable standards of consumption and have free access to education, health, pure water and information.

The tax system has favoured the rural areas while being progressive in respect of income. In terms of personal income the pre-1967 broadening of inequality has been halted, but even urban – rural inequality has been narrowed if access to public services is taken into account. The main policy tools are minimum wages, rural services and investment programmes and abolition of school fees and all direct taxes on increases below the minimum wage.[15] By 1975, for example, extension of pure water to villages was reaching at least 1,000,000 additional persons a year and a 1979 target for achieving water supply to all villages had been set. Similarly, by 1976 adult literacy in rural areas exceeded 50 per cent and about a third of the population were enrolled in adult-education programmes ranging from literacy to book-keeping and from political education to Swahili poetry.

The results of the ujamaa programme in organising the rural community to provide essential services and to manage their own development priorities and activities are positive and clear-cut. The programme has also made an important contribution to income redistribution in favour of the poorest segment of the population. But the production gains of the programme are not equally visible: 1973 and 1974 were marked by severe droughts and food production probably fell at least a tenth. However, in 1975 and 1976, weather was better with output in 1975 probably about equal to the 1972 peak and in 1976 significantly higher. Emphasis of the ujamaa programme has so far been on social relations and education. Facilities to increase inputs and technical knowledge are only now being expanded and should show up in production results in the next few years. But the average increase of about 3 per cent in agricultural (and food) production between 1967 and 1973 is ahead of the population growth and better than the average for Africa. It does not, however, provide the required margin of safety for bad-crop years like 1973 and 1974.

The creation of ujamaa villages and the accompanying policies of rural development in Tanzania have not been entirely smooth and free of problems. Many of the problems have been due to technical and managerial inadequacies: Tanzania did not have enough technical know-how in agriculture or managerial capacity and it has not been easy to train a large number of rural workers and cadres in a short time to mount a major programme for agricultural and rural development. Equally, it was also difficult to convert the local officials in rural areas from their roles of being rural elites to becoming the genuine servants of newly-created rural leadership. (It has been easier to persuade the central bureaucracy to participate in the transition to socialism and to accept cuts in their salaries.) As a result, neither the implementation of policies nor the provision of inputs and services by the Government has been uniformly efficient. Many farmers have been discouraged by contradictory instructions (for example, emphasis on maize in one year and on cotton cultivation in the next) and by unfulfilled promises (like guaranteed food supply if they would grow sisal on the collective farm).

One important factor which is gradually helping to overcome these problems and motivate and involve the local official is the role of the only political party – TANU – which has its own network of officials and local committees. The political strategy from the top also concentrates on a few critical and urgent problems, with support from limited technical and financial resources that are available, to solve these problems. In this way, the results are not dramatic and all-inclusive but essential political direction of social reforms and basic social change has been maintained with whatever economic progress can be realistically achieved.

To sum up, Tanzanian strategy for rural development illustrates the importance of building an egalitarian and healthy rural society through leadership, motivation and voluntary association, sharing equitably whatever resources are available and gradually increasing material and non-material facilities, rather than a rapid growth of agricultural production for its own sake. Tanzania's task in building such a society was facilitated by the virtual absence of landlords or a large privileged class in rural areas, but it required positive political leadership and guidance of the kind provided by President Nyerere and continuing support by a grass-root political party like TANU.

PUNJAB

The province of Punjab in India has an area of 50.400 square kilometres (5 million hectares), i.e. 1.5 per cent of the total area of the country, and a population of 13.55 million, i.e. 2.5 per cent of the country's total population. The population density per square kilometre in 1971 was 26.7 as compared to the national average of 18.2 per square kilometre.

Between 1950–1 and 1970–1, the agricultural output in Punjab has increased at a compound annual rate of 6.5 per cent, as compared to 3.3 per cent for India as a whole. The growth rate has been even more impressive in recent years. Between 1964–5 and 1970–1, the overall agricultural output has increased at a compound rate of 8.5 per cent and that of foodgrains at 10.6 per cent, as compared to 2.3 and 3.2 per cent respectively for the country as a whole. The average yield per hectare of wheat, rice and maize has increased during this period by 49, 44 and 24 per cent respectively:

Table C3 Production of Some Major Crops in Punjab (in 'ooo MT)

	1960–1	1964–5	1970–1	1971–2
Wheat	1742	2367	5145	5618
Rice	229	351	688	920
Maize	371	491	861	857
Sugar cane	486	445	527	403
Cotton	669	814	818	972
Oil seeds	121	220	233	272
Total cereals	2453	3342	6997	7623
Total foodgrains	3162	4028	7305	7925

(In percentage)

Compound growth rate between	Foodgrains	Non-foodgrains	All commodities
1950–1 and 1970–1	6.9 (3.5)	4.4 (2.7)	6.5 (3.3)
1950–1 and 1964–5	5.3 (3.7)	5.8 (3.7)	5.6 (3.7)
1964–5 and 1970–1	10.6 (3.2)	1.1 (0.4)	8.5 (2.3)

(Note: Figures in brackets are all-India growth rates)

From an annual deficit of 35,000 tons of foodgrains in the post-partition years, Punjab has emerged as a major food surplus area in India. Although it accounts for only 3 per cent of the total cultivated area in India, it now accounts for over 7 per cent of total foodgrains production in India and has been exporting over 2 million tons of foodgrains annually to other states in recent years.

One of the primary factors which has contributed to what is commonly referred to as 'Green Revolution' in the Punjab has been rapid expansion of irrigated area. The net irrigated area has increased by 37 per cent, from 2111 thousand hectares in 1964–5 to 2888 thousand hectares in 1970–1, and the area sown more than once has increased by 33 per cent from 1225 thousand hectares to 1625 thousand hectares during the same period. The bulk of this increase has been achieved through an expansion of private tube-wells, from 20,000 in 1966–7 to 113,500 in 1971–2.

Another major factor has been the impressive response of the Punjabi farmers to new agricultural technology. The area under high-yielding varieties of wheat, rice, maize and bajra has increased from 80 thousand hectares (i.e. 3 per cent of total area under these crops) in 1966–7 to over 2 million hectares (i.e. 62 per cent of the total area under the crops) in 1971–2. There has also been a marked increase in the consumption of fertilizers and pesticides. Total fertilizer consumption has increased from 258,000 tons in 1966–7 to 1,504,000 tons in 1970–1. The area covered by plant-protection operations has increased from 2 million hectares in 1966–7 to 4 million hectares in 1970–1. There has also been a marked increase in the number of tractors and other farm implements – the number of tractors has increased from 10,630 in 1966 to 23,200 in 1972.

Another important factor has been the land-tenure policy of the 1960s. There is a ceiling of 25 acres (10 hectares) on individual holdings and the Government has pursued an active policy for the consolidation of holdings. By 1968–9, almost the entire agricultural land had been consolidated into economically viable farm units. This has made the installation of tube-wells and adoption of new farm technology both viable and profitable. Partly as a result of the consolidation of holdings, the area under self-cultivation has increased remarkably in recent years and this has at least partly contributed to the rapid adoption of new technology in the State.

The expansion of co-operative services has made an equally important contribution by arranging timely procurement and distribution of fertilizers and pesticides and provision of adequate credit to the farmers for purchasing agricultural inputs and improving irrigation facilities. The Punjab State Co-operative Supply and Marketing Federation, with a network of 121 marketing societies and 4000 fertilizer depots at village level, have continued to maintain the supply of fertilizers in spite of periodical shortages.

By 1970–1 the number of active primary agricultural societies in Punjab was 10,189 covering almost 99 per cent of the villages. The average deposits per society and per member in 1970–1 were Rs 17,262 and Rs 123 respectively as compared to Rs 4320 and Rs 22 for India as a whole. Total advances granted by these societies were Rs 570 million, and the average loans per society and per member were Rs 55,575 and Rs 529 respectively as compared to Rs 35,938 and Rs 514 for the country.

Equally important has been the Government policy of supporting prices for farm products, which have steadily increased during the 1960s. Between 1959–62 and 1972 the index of wholesale prices of twenty-one agricultural commodities has more than doubled. This, coupled with the Government's price-support policy, has provided a strong incentive to the farmers to maximise their farm production. Correspondingly, rural wages in Punjab were at least twice as large as in the rest of the country and this has attracted substantial migration of seasonal workers to the Punjab.

Punjab, with its impressive record of agricultural progress, is one of the most successful examples of the 'intermediate' approaches to rural development mentioned in Chapter 8. A hard-working and intelligent population with a good agricultural base can achieve sustained increments in production and incomes if it has access to improved technology, credit and essential agricultural inputs such as fertilizers and tube-wells and their efforts are backed by an active land tenure policy, with a ceiling on large holdings and consolidation of small holdings, price-support operations and improved social services. It can even increase employment opportunities in agro industries and other activities generated by rapid agricultural progress. But with a cultivable area of 5 million hectares for a rural population of 10 million, even a ceiling of 10 hectares for private holdings will leave 20–25 per cent of the rural population without any land holdings. Rapid agricultural progress could provide employment to some of these landless people but their share in the total income cannot be prevented from declining.

According to a recent study,[16] during a period of very rapid growth in agriculture there was an improvement in the mean per capita consumption of the rural population but there was an absolute decline in the consumption levels of the poorest 30 per cent of the population. Assuming a per capita monthly consumption of Rs 16.36 (about US$ 2.0) as the poverty line for the region as a whole, the percentage of population living below this

Table C4 Percentages of population lying below selected absolute levels of per capita monthly consumption, 1960–1 and 1970–1

Per capita monthly consumption level 1960–1 prices (Rs.)	Per cent population poorer in 1960–1	Equivalent consumption level, 1970–1 prices [1] (Rs.)	Per cent population poorer in 1970–1
11.66	5.00	24.14	6.32
14.31	10.00	29.62	12.36
15.72	15.00	32.52	20.52
16.36[2]	18.40	33.86	23.28
16.66	20.00	34.49	24.95
17.13	25.00	35.46	26.90
17.86	30.00	36.97	30.02

1. The price index of 2.0696 was used uniformly for all consumption levels since the population considered here falls entirely within the poorest fractile group.
2. The poverty line constructed for the region. Details of its construction are available in Rajaraman (1974).

line increased from 18.40 to 23.28 per cent.

Perhaps the political and cultural obstacles for changing the pattern of ownership or for improving the lot of the poorest 30 per cent are insurmountable. Perhaps, considering the political and economic situation of India, the results achieved in the Punjab reflect one the best examples of an 'intermediate' solution, but as a model of rural development one cannot ignore its limitations in achieving the longer-term objectives of abolishing the poverty of the poorest segments and harmonising social relations in the society.

Notes and References

INTRODUCTION

1. IBRD/IDS: *Redistribution with Growth*; Joint Study by the World Bank's Development Research Center and the Institute of Development Studies, University of Sussex (Oxford University Press, 1974).

CHAPTER I

1. Joseph Needham, 'The Past in China's Present', *Pacific Viewpoint*, 4, 2 (September 1963).
2. These and subsequent figures in this chapter are based on Dwight H. Perkin's work, *Agricultural Development in China* (Edinburgh University Press, 1969).
3. Jan Myrdal, *Report from a Chinese Village* (Pelican Books, 1967) p. 184.
4. William Hinton, *Fanshen, A Documentary of Revolution in a Chinese Village* (Vintage Books, 1966).
5. Briefing given to the author in February 1973 by Mr Chen Chung, Director, Bureau of Agriculture, Ministry of Agriculture and Forestry.
6. In a recent article, 'Surplus and Stagnation in Modern China', Carl Riskin has calculated on the basis of 1935 data that the Chinese economy had an actual surplus of 27 per cent of net domestic product and was capable of adding another 10 percentage points by producing to its potential but this surplus was not used in growth-inducing ways. It served to feed privileged consumption habits, hypertrophic bureaucracies and foreign appetites. In *China's Modern Economy in Historical Perspective*, ed. Dwight H. Perkins (Stanford University Press, 1975).

CHAPTER 2

1. This criteria was first explained by Mao Tse-tung in a document written in October 1933 and was adopted by the 'Workers and Peasants Democratic Central Government' of that time. The

document is published in vol. 1 of the *Selected Works of Mao Tse-tung* (Peking, Foreign Languages Press, 1967).

2. Benedict Stavis in his forthcoming book *The Politics of Agricultural Mechanization in China* (Cornell University Press, 1977) has estimated, after evaluating various estimates of the extent of violence in land reforms, that officially 'about 400,000 to 800,000 "counter-revolutionaries" were killed between 1949 and 1951. The number killed unofficially cannot be known. Landlords constituted only a fraction of those executed. . . . Moreover, the violence and loss of life inherent in revolutionary land reform should be compared with the violence and loss of life in the "normal" situation.'

3. The landlords and their sons and daughters even after their 'absorption' in the new structure were observed carefully to guard against any reactionary tendencies among them. Except those whose exemplary behaviour had proved their bona fide, the rest were regarded as 'bad elements', denied positions of responsibility and supervised by local cadres.

4. Cheng Shuh, *A Glance at China's Economy* (Peking, Foreign Languages Press, 1974).

5. Incidentally, the term 'People's Commune' was not coined by the Government or the Party leadership. In what is now Chiliying People's Commune, four advanced co-operatives had volunteered in 1957 to merge to build a canal jointly with a labour force of 2000. Encouraged by the success of this merger, in July 1958, fifty-six advanced co-operatives in Chiliyings' thirty-eight villages applied to the county through the Party Committee at Hsiang level for permission to merge. This merger was approved on 4 July and was called 'Red Flag Federation of Co-operatives'. On 4 August, inspired by the term 'Paris Commune' of 1871, they changed the name to 'People's Commune'. Chairman Mao visited this Commune on 6 August 1958 and said 'That is a good name'. The term was subsequently adopted by the Central Committee of the Party.

6. See extract from Chairman Mao's article of July 1955 'On the Question of Agricultural Co-operation' reproduced in Chapter 3 (page 22).

7. It seems that the policy of enlarging the size of the commune was again introduced after the Cultural Revolution in 1966 – 7. During my fourth visit to China in August 1975, an official of the Ministry of Agriculture told me that the total number of communes was now 50,000.

8. 'Communique of the 10th Plenary Session of the 8th Central Committee of the Chinese Communist Party', NCNA Peking, 28 September 1962.

9. A partial analysis of the Socialist Education Movement, essentially as a commentary on the goals and techniques of mass campaigns in China, is presented by Richard Baum in 'Prelude to Revolution', *Mao, the Party and the Peasant Question 1962–1966* (Columbia University Press, 1975).

CHAPTER 3

1. Mao Tse-tung, *On The Question of Agricultural Co-operation* (Peking: Foreign Languages Press, 1956).
2. Mao Tse-tung, *On the Correct Handling of Contradiction among the People* (Peking: Foreign Languages Press, 1960).
3. The English text of this Programme was published by the Foreign Languages Press, Peking, in 1956 under the title *The Draft Programme for Agricultural Development in The People's Republic of China*. A second, revised version was adopted in October 1957, and a final version adopted in April 1960, whose text is available in *Communist China 1955–1959* (Harvard University Press, Cambridge, Mass., 1962) pp. 1–17. Changes from one version to the other are not substantial.
4. Mao Tse-tung, *Sixty Work Methods (Draft)*, 31 January 1958. This document has not so far been officially published by the Chinese authorities. These and subsequent quotations are based on an unofficial version dated 19 February 1958.
5. See, for example, Benedict Stavis, *Making Green Revolution – The Politics of Agricultural Development in China* (Ithaca, New York: Cornell Center for International Studies, 1974), updated in Benedict Stavis, 'A Preliminary Model for Grain Production in China: 1974, *China Quarterly* (January 1976). In the latter article, Stavis has estimated 'new or improved irrigated and drained region to be 33 million hectares', mechanised area at 25 million hectares and area sown to very high yielding varieties at 10.9 million hectares.
6. Source: Jingji Yanjiu, *Economic Research*, No. 7 (July 1965), in Tregear, *An Economic Geography of China* (London: Butterworths, 1970) p. 72.
7. Sources: 1952: *Ten Great Years* (English edition, Peking, 1960) p. 128. 1975: Author's own estimate based on semi-official briefing.
8. Cheng Shih, *A Glance at China's Economy* (Peking: Foreign Languages Press, 1974) p. 17.
9. This relatively simple improvement in rice-cultivation practices – shortening the growing period – could be of great potential significance, particularly for rice-growing Asian count-

ries. In India, for example, only 20 per cent of the total cultivated area of 140 million hectares is double cropped. This is mainly because rice is planted in nurseries only after the rains start in June, transplanted in July–August and harvested in December when it is too late to plant wheat or another winter crop. If groups of farmers could be persuaded to prepare rice nurseries with tubewell water even before the rains start, they could be transplanted and harvested four weeks earlier, allowing at least half the rice acreage of 40 million hectares to grow another crop. This factor alone, it has been estimated, could increase India's grain output by 20 per cent, and much more if simultaneous use is made of better seed varieties and organic manures in conjunction with chemical fertilizers.

10. Detailed estimates for the period 1952 and 1966 given by Kang Chao, *Agricultural Production in Communist China* (Wisconsin University Press, 1970). The figures for 1972 are estimated by Benedict Stavis, *Making Green Revolution* (Cornell University, 1974). According to Chao, in 1966, about 33 per cent of the natural fertilizer was obtained from night soil, 20 per cent from large animal manures, 18 per cent from pig manure, 14 per cent from green manure, 8 per cent from oilseed cakes, 4 per cent from plant residue compost and the remaining 3 per cent from rivers, ponds and other sources.

11. F.A.O., *Statistics of Crops Responses to Fertilizers* (1966).

12. In Tachai, the famous production brigade in Shensi Province, they have obtained an average yield of 7.5 tons per hectare for maize, the same as the best hybrid maize in the United States but with only about one-third of chemical fertilizer compared with that used in the United States. This is because the brigade uses 40–5 tons of organic manure per hectare by mixing maize stalk compost with pig manure which is equivalent to about 150 kg of plant nutrient per hectare.

13. According to one report, the utilisation of walking tractors in one production brigade in Kiangsu has increased from 600 hours per year in 1971 to 2400 hours in 1973: New China News Agency, 29 August 1974: Selection from PRC Press: American Consulate, Hong Kong, 1974, 37 p. 104.

14. New China News Agency, Peking, *Domestic Service* (20 October 1975). Also reproduced in *The China Quarterly* (London: March 1976), and published by the Foreign Languages Press, Peking in 1975, along with excerpts from other speeches made at the Conference.

15. Another Agricultural Conference was held in Peking in December 1976 to consolidate and re-emphasise the message of the Conference held in October 1975. See page 85.

CHAPTER 4

1. In China's socialist system four kinds of ownership were distinguished in the constitution approved in 1954: private, communal, co-operative and State. Private ownership was confined to small tools, private rural dwellings, some urban housing and very small plots of land (but these cannot be sold). Communal ownership included all land in rural communities, all means of agricultural production and commune-owned industries. Co-operative ownership covered mainly means of production or services in non-rural communities, like trade or processing, and membership was linked only to employment. State ownership extended to all land not owned by the commune and to all means of production not owned by the commune or the co-operative. A new constitution adopted in 1974, however, recognised only two kinds of ownership: '*socialist* ownership by the whole people' and 'socialist ownership by labouring masses'. The former refers to State ownership and the latter to communal ownership.

2. It is not clear whether this reduction in the number of communes represents a one-time rationalisation or reflects a continuing process of enlarging the size of the commune. It is presumably the former and resulted from the amalgamation of many small and scattered communes in remote areas. In most of what is agricultural China, the present commune size covering the traditional area of the old market town has justified its institutional viability. Bigger projects (like the Red Flag Canal) or sophisticated industries (like tractor manufacture) have in practice been taken up at the county level.

3. In 1958, when communes were first established, the average number of households in each of the 26,000 communes was officially reported to be 4635 (*Ten Great Years*, op. cit. p. 43). Since then, with a 40 per cent increase in population, and an estimated 20 per cent increase in the number of households, the average number of households in each of the 50,000 communes would work out to about 3000.

4. See Chapter 3, p. 27.

5. In China, after the Cultural Revolution, the process of strengthening the skilled manpower in rural areas was taken a step further and many high-school graduates were sent to rural areas for work. A certain proportion of these educated youths (Zhi Shi Qing nian) can go back for college or university education on the recommendation of the commune leaders or to factory jobs in the cities, but the rest stay on in rural areas, depending on 'socialist requirements'.

6. Some brigades have also begun experimenting with certain variations of the Tachai system. For example, in the Liu Chuang Brigade of Chiliying Commune, Hunan Province, I was told, every member received ¥40 a year (¥18 in cash) as a minimum, irrespective of the amount of work done. Only the rest of the income is distributed according to work points. Total collective income distributed among 1200 members of this brigade in 1974 was ¥175,000 which was 40 per cent of the gross income of the brigade. The total per capita average income that year was ¥150.

7. Members of the Ma Lu Commune, near Shanghai, with a population of 7000 households (and a total population of 28,000), which I visited in 1975, had 5193 bicycles, 5727 watches and 1312 sewing machines. They also had forty-seven doctors, fifty-nine barefoot doctors and 179 health workers.

8. Article 16 of *Sixty Work Methods*, referred to in Chapter 3 (p. 24), deals with this subject in the following manner: 'The question of the ratio of accumulation to consumption in agricultural co-operatives must also be studied. Comrades of Hupeh are of the view that the production and distribution figures of 1957 should be taken as the base and subsequent increase of production should be divided at the ratio of 4:6 (that is 40 per cent for distribution to commune members and 60 per cent for use as co-operative accumulation), half and half, or at the ratio of 4:6 in the reverse order. If production and income have reached the level of the well-off peasants of the place, after airing of views and discussion and subject to the consent of the masses, part of the increased output may be divided at the ratio of 3:7'

CHAPTER 5

1. According to the United Nations 1973 estimate, China's birthrate is twenty-seven per 1000, and death rate ten per 1000 with a rate of natural increase of 1.7 per annum. A more recent estimate by the Worldwatch Institute, Washington DC (*Worldwatch Paper 8* (October 1976)) puts the birthrate at nineteen per 1000, death rate at eight yielding a natural rate of increase of only 1.1 per cent.

2. The corresponding figures for some other developing Asian countries for 1975 are: India, 196; Pakistan, 194; Indonesia, 198; Sri Lanka, 186; Thailand, 332. *Source*: FAO Food Balance Sheets (1975).

3. The eating habits and culinary traditions of China, reflecting their age-old wisdom, have also contributed to better nutrition. Unlike the average Western citizen, the Chinese do not consume much fat

and sugar, and for protein they rely more on soya-bean, poultry and pigs than on beef.

4. See note 1 above.

5. The term 'man' is used here in a generic sense and includes all men and women. So is the term 'he' used subsequently.

6. The Cultural Revolution was steeped in the idea that bureaucrats can create class antagonism and thus departed from the Marxian thought that they would 'wither away'.

7. *Selected works of Mao Tse-Tung*, vol. 1 (Peking: Foreign Languages Press, 1967).

8. For a further discussion of this aspect of China, see Johan Galtung and Gumiko Nishimura, *Learning from the Chinese People* (1976) Chapter 2.

9. Joint Economic Committee, U.S. Congress, *China – a Re-assessment of the Economy* (Washington D.C., 1975).

10. Quoted by John Gittings in 'New Light on China's Political Economy', *IDS Bulletin* (August 1975). See note 1 of Chapter 6.

11. According to some recent studies there has been a definite reduction in inter-regional inequality in China between 1952 and 1971. Unlike the experience of most other countries with an inverted U-shaped pattern of regional distribution of income, in China the reduction of inter-regional inequality began simultaneously with a sustained increase in per capita GDP growth. This has been achieved through intensified industrial activity in less-developed areas, since the per capita agricultural income has been unevenly distributed from the outset. See Nicholas R. Lardy, *Regional Growth and Income Distribution: The Chinese Experience*, presented to the Research Conference on the Lessons of China's Development Experience for the Developing Countries, Hyatt Puerto Rico, San Juan, Puerto Rico, 1976; Economic Growth Center, Yale University.

12. The speech by Chen Yung Kuei, the founder and first Party Secretary of Tachai Brigade, and now Vice Premier of State Council, is reproduced in *Peking Review* of 7 January 1977, and the closing address of Chairman Hua Kuo-Feng on 25 December 1976 has been published as a supplement to *China Reconstructs*.

CHAPTER 6

1. This collection is in two volumes (of 280 and 720 pages) written in 1959–60, under the title *Long Live Mao Tse-tung's Thought*. It includes his speech on the book *Economic Problems of Socialism* and 'Reading Notes on the Soviet Textbook – Political Economy'. Other

documents deal with the Great Leap Forward, the Socialist Education Movement and the Cultural Revolution. The collection has not so far been released but an unofficial version is published as *Miscellany of Mao Tse-tung's Thought* by Joint Publication Research Service, Arlington, Virginia (1974) (No. JPRS/61269/1-2). A useful summary of the main points extracted from Mao's *Notes on Political Economy* is presented by John Gittings in *IDS Bulletin* (August 1975).

2. A. O. Hirschman, *The Strategy of Economic Development* (New Haven: Yale University Press, 1958). Hirschman sees development as a chain of disequilibria in which larger demand for one product based on past investment induces complementary demand for other products, leading to new investment and many positive external economies.

3. Lenin's initial stress on collectivisation, it is interesting to recall, was based on technical considerations related to economies of scale arising from the need for large-scale mechanisation of agriculture. V. Lenin, *Development of Capitalism in Russia* (Progress Publishers, 1967). The term 'collectivisation' is used here in a more generic sense and should not be confused with the Russian experiment of collectivisation in the 1930s.

CHAPTER 7

1. IBRD / IDS, *Redistribution with Growth*, op. cit. See Introduction, page xvi.
2. B. S. Minhas, 'Rural Poverty, Land Distribution and Development Strategy: Policy', *The Indian Journal of Statistics*, vol. 6 (1974) p. 399.
3. Government of Pakistan, *Master Survey of Agriculture* (1970) Table 1.

CHAPTER 8

1. In some ways the essence of this approach reflects the philosophies of Gandhi and David Thoreau and their strong belief in the ultimate superiority and victory of a just and moral cause pursued through a firm but non-violent struggle.
2. *Rural Development*, Sector Policy Paper, International Bank for Reconstruction and Development (February 1975). The strategy calls for a considerable increase in total World Bank lending in agriculture with an increasing share for the poorest countries and for poverty-oriented projects. It estimates the external investment requirements for a 'major attack on rural poverty' at $10 billion a year (against $2 billion in 1975).

APPENDIX C

1. R. P. Sinha has argued that in terms of pre-modern agricultural technology there was not much difference between India and China in the late 1940s or early 1950s and Japan in the 1870s. See R. P. Sinha, 'Competing Ideology and Agricultural Strategy: Current Agricultural Development in India and China compared with Meiji Strategy', in *World Development*, vol. I, No. 6 (June 1973).

2. (*a*) J. Nakmara, *Agricultural Production and the Economic Development of Japan 1873–1922* (Princeton University Press, 1966).
   (*b*) K. Ohkawa, B. F. Johnston and H. Kaneda, *Agriculture and Economic Growth: Japan's Experience* (University of Tokyo Press, 1969).
   (*c*) T. Okura, *Agricultural Development in Modern Japan* (Tokyo, 1963).

3. R. P. Dore, 'Agricultural Improvement in Japan 1870–1900', *Economic Development and Cultural Change*, vol. IX, 1 (1960).

4. Shigeru Ishikawa and Kazushi Ohkawa, 'Significance of Japan's Experience – Technological Changes in Agricultural Production and Changes in Agrarian Structure', in *Agriculture and Economic Development*, Papers and Proceedings of a Conference held by The Japan Economic Research Center (6–10 September 1971), vol. I, The Japan Economic Research Center (May 1972).

5. In 1964, the average number of settlers in a kibbutz was 358 and only a few large settlements with a population of over 1000. See Michael Frank, *Co-operative Land Settlements in Israel and their Relevance to African Countries* (Kyklos-Verlag Basel, JCB Mohr, Tübingen, 1968) p. 22.

6. For a more detailed description of the kibbutz, see E. Kannovsky, 'The Economy of the Israeli Kibbutz', *Harvard Middle Eastern Monograph No. 13* (Harvard University, 1966). Also see M. Frank, 1968, op. cit.

7. For a more detailed account of the moshav, see M. Frank, op. cit. Also See A. Rokach, 'The Kibbutz and the Moshav', *UNESCO Arid Zone Research No. 23*.

8. The annual increase of 8.8 per cent in agricultural production (12.1 per cent during 1952–62 and 5.4 per cent in 1962–71) means a fivefold increase in total agricultural production over these twenty years. This was achieved with only 20 per cent increase in cultivable land mainly because of a 184 per cent increase in water availability and 226 per cent increase in the supply of capital. See Israel, *CBS Annual Abstracts of Israel, Jerusalem, and Census of Agriculture, 1971*, Preliminary Data (Jerusalem, 1972).

9. Some other countries of East Europe, like Poland, have achieved impressive results in agriculture without collectivising the ownership of land. The bulk of land is owned privately but 95 per cent of all production means are provided by service co-operatives and 90 per cent of total agricultural output is marketed through co-operatives. There is also no significant difference in average yields between State, Co-operative farms or private farms. In general, those East European countries which started with bigger holdings per farmer, more capital per hectare and more advanced skills and knowledge, have been able to move forward to a greater degree of collectivisation in agriculture. Some others, like Poland and Yugoslavia, have achieved equally good results by encouraging service co-operatives while retaining private ownership.

10. The Youth Wing of the Tanganyika African National Union (TANU), the only political party before independence, had experimented with self-help settlements even prior to independence. The experience gained from these experiments helped shape the Ujamaa concept.

11. *United Republic of Tanzania, Second Five Year Plan for Economic and Social Development*, vol. 1 (Government Printer, Dar-es-Salaam, 1969) p. 26.

12. J. K. Nyerere, 'Socialism and Rural Development'. This was the second most important post-Arusha paper released in September 1967, and is published in Nyerere, *Freedom and Socialism* (Dar-es-Salaam: Oxford University Press, 1968).

13. *Second Five Year Plan*, op. cit.

14. Government of Republic of Tanzania Agriculture Census: 1972. Preliminary Results.

15. R. H. Green, 'Toward Ujamaa and Kujitegemea: Income Distribution and Absolute Poverty Eradication: Aspects of the Tanzania Transition to Socialism', *IDS Discussion Paper*, No. 66 (December 1974).

16. Indira Rajaraman, 'Poverty, Inequality and Economic Growth: Rural Punjab 1960/61 – 1970/71, *Journal of Development Studies*.

Bibliography

Richard Baum, 'Prelude to Revolution', in *Mao, the Party and the Peasant Question 1962–1966* (New York: Columbia University Press, 1975).

Charles Bettelheim, *Cultural Revolution and Industrial Organization in China – Changes in Management and the Division of Labour* (New York: Monthly Review Press, 1974).

Keith Buchanan, *The Transformation of the Chinese Earth: Aspects of the Evaluation of the Chinese Earth from Earliest Times to Mao Tse-tung* (London: Bell, 1970).

Kang Chao, *Agricultural Production in Communist China 1949–1965* (Madison: University of Wisconsin Press, 1970).

Hollis Chenery, Introduction to *Redistribution with Growth*. A joint study by the World Bank's Development Research Centre and IDS in the United Kingdom (Oxford University Press, 1974).

Shih Chen, *A Glance at China's Economy* (Peking: Foreign Languages Press, 1974).

R. P. Dore, 'Agricultural Improvement in Japan 1870–1900', *Economic Development and Cultural Change*, vol. IX, 1 (1960).

A. Eckstein, *Communist China's Economic Growth and Foreign Trade* (New York: McGraw-Hill, 1966).

Gilbert Etienne, *La Voie Chinoise; la longue marche de l'économie 1949–1974* (Paris: Presses Universitaires de France (Collection Tiers Monde), 1974).

C. P. Fitzgerald, *Floodside in China* (London: Cresset, 1958).

Food and Agriculture Organisation, *Statistics of Crops Responses to Fertilizers* (1966).

Michael Frank, *Cooperative Land Settlements in Israel and their Relevance to African Countries* (Tübingen: Kyklos-Verlag Basel, JCB Mohr, 1968).

J. Gittings, 'New Light on China's Political Economy', *IDS Bulletin*, vol. 7, 2 (August 1975).

Government of Pakistan, *Master Survey of Agriculture 1970*.

J. Gray, 'The Two Roads: Alternative Strategies of Social Change and Economic Growth in China', in S. R. Schram (ed.), *Authority, Participation and Cultural Change in China* (Cambridge: Cambridge University Press, 1973).

R. H. Green, 'Toward Ujamaa and Kujitegemea: Income Distribution and Absolute Poverty Eradication: Aspects of the Tanzania Transition to Socialism', *IDS Discussion Paper* No. 66 (December 1974).

W. Hinton, 'Awaken the Mountains, Let the Rivers Change their Face . . .', *New China*, 1(1) (New York, Spring 1975).

W. Hinton, *Fanshen: A Documentary of Revolution in a Chinese Village* (New York: Vintage Books, 1966).

A. O. Hirschman, *The Strategy of Economic Development* (New Haven: Yale University Press, 1958).

Israel CBS Abstracts of Israel, Jerusalem and Census of Agriculture, *1971 Preliminary Data* (Jerusalem, 1972).

The Japan Economic Research Center, *Agriculture and Economic Development* (Tokyo, May 1972).

E. Kannovsky, 'The Economy of the Israeli Kibbutz', *Harvard Middle Eastern Monograph Series*, No. 13 (Cambridge: Harvard University Press, 1966).

L. T. C. Kuo, *The Technical Transformation of Agriculture in Communist China* (New York: Praeger, 1972).

N. R. Lardy, *Regional Growth and Income Distribution: The Chinese Experience*. Presented to a Research Conference on the Lessons of China's Development Experience for the Developing Countries, sponsored by the Sub-Committee on Research on the Chinese Economy of the SSRC–ACLS Joint Committee on Contemporary China (San Juan, Puerto Rico, 1976).

V. Lenin, *Development of Capitalism in Russia* (London: Lawrence and Wishart Ltd, 1957).

A. W. Lewis, 'Economic Development with Unlimited Supplies of Labour', *Manchester School*, vol. 22 (May 1954).

Mao Tse-tung, *Selected Works*, 4 volumes (Peking: Foreign Languages Press, 1967).

——, *On the Correct Handling of Contradictions Among the People* (Peking: Foreign Languages Press, 1960).

——, *On the Question of Agricultural Co-operation* (Peking: Foreign Languages Press, 1956).

B. S. Minhas, 'Rural Poverty, Land Distribution and Development Strategy: Policy', *The Indian Journal of Statistics*, vol. 6 (1974).

J. Myrdal, *Report from a Chinese Village* (Harmondsworth: Penguin Books, 1967).

J. Nakmara, *Agricultural Production and the Economic Development of Japan 1873–1922* (Princeton: Princeton University Press, 1966).

J. Needham, 'The Past in China's Present', *Pacific Viewpoint*, vol. 4, 2 (1963).

New China News Agency, *Communiqué of the 10th Plenary Session of the 8th*

Central Committee of the Chinese Communist Party (Peking, September 1962).

P. Nurkse, *Problems of Capital Formation in Underdeveloped Countries* (Oxford: Basil Blackwell, 1953).

J. K. Nyrere, *Freedom and Socialism* (Dar-es-Salaam: Oxford University Press, 1968).

K. Ohkawa, B. F. Johnston and H. Kaneda, *Agriculture and Economic Growth, Japan's Experience* (Tokyo: University of Tokyo Press, 1969).

T. Okura, *Agricultural Development in Modern Japan* (Tokyo, 1963).

D. H. Perkins, *Agricultural Development in China* (Edinburgh: Edinburgh University Press, 1969).

——, *The Central Features of China's Economic Development*. Paper presented to a Research Conference on the Lessons of China's Development Experience for the Developing Countries. Sponsored by the Sub-Committee on Research on the Chinese Economy of the SSRC–ACLS Joint Committee on Contemporary China (San Juan, Puerto Rico, January 1976).

C. Riskin, 'Surplus and Stagnation in Modern China', in D. H. Perkins (ed.), *China's Modern Economy in Historical Perspective* (Stanford: Stanford University Press, 1975).

J. Robinson, *Economic Management 1974* (London: Anglo-Chinese Educational Institute, 1975).

A. Rokach, 'The Kibbutz and the Moshav', *UNESCO Arid Zone Research*, No. 23 (1964).

J. L. Sampedro, *Decisive Forces in World Economics* (London: World University Press, 1967).

I. Shigeru and O. Kazushi, 'Significance of Japan's Experience – Technological Changes in Agricultural Production and Changes in Agrarian Structure', in *Agriculture and Economic Development*. Papers and Proceedings of a Conference held by the Japan Economic Research Center, 6–10 September 1971, vol. 1 (The Japan Economic Center, May 1972).

R. P. Sinha, 'Competing Ideology and Agricultural Strategy: Current Agricultural Development in India and China Compared with Meiji Strategy', *World Development*, vol. 1, 6 (June 1973).

B. Stavis, *Making Green Revolution – The Politics of Agricultural Development in China*, The Cornell East Asia Monograph Series No. 1 (Ithaca: Cornell University Press, 1974).

T. R. Tregear, *An Economic Geography of China* (London: Butterworths, 1970).

United Nations Population Division, 'World Population 1970–2000', ESA/P/W 1. 53 (10 March 1975).

United Republic of Tanzania, *Second Five Year Plan for Economic and*

Social Development, vol. 1 (Dar-es-Salaam: Government Printer, 1969).

United States Congress Joint Economic Committee (ed.), *China: A Reassessment of the Economy* (Washington, D.C.: U.S. Government Printing Office, 10 July 1975).

K. Walker, *Planning in Chinese Agriculture: Socialisation and the Private Sector, 1956–1962* (London: Cass, 1965).

World Bank, *Rural Development*. Sector Policy Paper (February 1975).

Jingj Xue Jichu Zhishi Zhengzhi, *Basic Knowledge in the Study of Political Economy* (Shanghai: People's Press, 1974).

Index

The plates are positioned between pp. 58 and 59; references to plates are given below as *58**.